Satan

CAN BE STOPPED!

Releasing the unstoppable power of the Kingdom of God through prayer

TODD SMITH

SATAN CAN BE STOPPED
By Todd Smith
Copyright © Todd Smith

Cover Design: Marty Darracott
Editor: Dana Fowler

DEDICATION

I dedicate this book to my grandchildren, Sutton, Bo, Cooper.

The world you live in now is dangerous, unpredictable, and ever shifting toward deeper darkness. The three of you have been strategically given to this era and your specific generation. You were born to FIND Him, LOVE Him, SHARE Him and DISPLAY Him.

I want you to take comfort in this one fact, each of you will be used of the Lord to bring a bright light to a wicked world. If you learn to pray you will be unstoppable - you will conquer and win. Angels will respond to your slightest whisper and your softest request. Prayer will be your greatest battle, the devil will do all within his power to keep you from it. However, if you learn to pray effectively you will move mountains, slay giants, split seas, curse fig trees, silence Jezebels, and feed the multitudes.

It will be your highest calling! The passion of my heart is that you learn to pray!

Sincerely,
Pops

INTRODUCTION

Augustine,"I count myself one of the number of those who write as they learn and learn as they write." Over the last several years I have learned a great deal about personal and corporate prayer. In the pages to follow is my feeble attempt to unpack the power of fervent prevailing prayer. I have written what I have learned from personal experience as well from the experience and practices of others.

Arthur Wallis said, "At the heart of every revival is the spirit of prayer." Revival feeds on prayer. If prayer is present and fervent the revival intensifies, however, the revival will shrivel if it is not nourished appropriately and consistently with prayer. We must pray!

THIS IS WHAT I KNOW...Prayer is sacred, and delicate and yet wild and violent. At times you feel alone and then the next you sense the the very presence of the God in the room. Prayer in its purest since is designed to encounter God, to hear Him speak, feel His touch, receive His correction, walk in His guidance, and to rest in His goodness, and so much more.

Prayer affords an encounter with the living God that moves Him to action. It summons the angels and hand of God into our time and space.

TABLE OF CONTENTS

1

WHAT WILL BE YOUR STORY?

"God's cause is committed to men; God commits Himself to men. Praying men are the vice-regents of God; they do His work and carry out His plans".
E.M. Bounds

One of the greatest impacts on my life was attending the Brownsville Revival in Pensacola, Florida. The Pensacola Outpouring, as it became known, touched the world. There were three primary leaders: Pastor John Kilpatrick, Evangelist Steve Hill, and Worship Leader Lindell Cooley.

A few years after the revival ended, each of the men went their separate ways. Steve Hill planted a new church in Dallas, Texas. Lindell Cooley was preaching in the Dallas area and reached out to Steve to see if he had a few minutes so they could reunite, talk, and fellowship together.

Steve said, "Yes, I have some time this afternoon. Swing on by." Lindell drove to Steve's office, and they talked. But during the conversation, only as Steve could do, he pulls out a picture and sets it on the table in front of Lindell.

Steve with an inquisitive tone said, "Do you see that Lindell?"

Lindell responded, "What is it?"

Steve replied, "It's a young Muslim boy being baptized!"

The picture was a young man, 17-18 years old, being baptized.

Steve said, "Do you know something peculiar about the picture?" Lindell said, "No." Steve encouraged him to look again for the picture wasn't really close.

"Oh, Steve! He doesn't have any arms!" Lindell proclaimed.

At this point, Steve began to cry. He said, "Lindell, his arms were cut off because he professed Jesus. His family cut his arms off because he professed Jesus!"

Steve added, "Lindell, I want to ask you something. What if when we get to heaven at the marriage supper of the Lamb and you sit across the table from that young man and he looks at you and says, *"TELL ME YOUR STORY."*

What is *your* story? What would *you* say? What would *you* dare communicate to the young boy who had his arms cut off because he loved Jesus more than anything? More than even his arms!

We better have a story!!!

Be honest with yourself. What would you say if the young man asked to hear your story about how you served, sacrificed, and lived for Jesus?

WHAT WILL WE SAY? That we made a lot of money? That we had a nice career. That we worked hard so our families can have things...

I lived in a nice home... I gave and supported a missionary once... I went to church pretty regularly... I tithed...I prayed every now and then when I could get there... I did the best I could....

This young man's sacrifice and commitment to Jesus should motivate us to work on OUR STORY.

There is an interesting passage of scripture in Psalms where King David said, *"So teach us to number our days, That we may gain a heart of wisdom,"* (Psalm 90:12).

How much time do you have left? This is a sobering question. Go ahead and calculate how many days you think you have left on the earth. If you think you have 10 years of productive time left to serve the Lord that means you 3,650 days left. Wow! This puts into perspective that we must be "about our Father's business." We have to work on our story. We must aggressively seize the moment and the days we have left...there is no time to waste.

I desperately want you to have a story to tell.

This book is written to help you construct your story. In fact, one of the best ways to develop your story is committing yourself to be an instrument of prayer. Why will this matter? It is here in the battle field of prayer that you will do your greatest damage to the enemy and at the same time you will affect people, lands and nations for the Kingdom of God. It is here that you will move mountains and men.

Every soldier who has fought in a war has a story (or many stories) to tell. It comes with the territory. They vividly remember smells, images, and encounters. As soon as a recruit takes the oath of service and puts on the uniform, his life experiences change. He will be forever marked by his time in the military.

THIS IS WHAT I KNOW!

God is recruiting you now into the vast growing army of intercessors. You have a role to play, and that role is significant. All He needs is your "YES!" If you give it to Him, then everything changes from that point forward.

I can't wait to hear your story!

2

THIS IS NOT THE SAME DEVIL

"Oh God, rather than trying to convince preachers to pray, moving forward may you only call praying men/women to preach."
Todd Smith

You don't have to have a seminary degree to realize we are in an epic spiritual and natural battle with demonic forces. In these end times, I strongly feel we are dealing with an entirely different species of demons. These ferocious demons have been released in this hour to assault the work and people of God.

I don't want this to discourage you, but I do want to awaken you so you can be a part of the greatest harvest season the Church has ever seen. The response to the devil's activity has to change. What we have done will not get the job done. Here is the response: PRAYER! Prayer is the antidote to all of satan's activities.

Eric Ludy says it best, "You see, in God's economy, things on this Earth do not change through wishing, through positive thinking, or through good karma. They change through faith expressing itself in loving fervent prayer. God's people are commissioned to ask, to seek, to knock and to plead the realities of heaven be made reality down here on Earth."[1]

This is the way Jesus taught us to pray, "Lord, your kingdom come and your will be done on earth as it is in heaven." We don't need to *simply* pray; we need to *extraordinarily* pray. Why? The days we live in now are anything but safe and ordinary. Again, it is breathtaking at the ferocity and veraciousness that darkness is advancing in our world. Each and every day it seems things are compounding and getting worse. In order for things to improve and change we have to match the intensity of darkness with a greater intensity of prayer. We have to adjust our engagement in prayer to meet the level of darkness in our society. It is no longer an option; we must practice prevailing prayer.

---

[1] Eric Ludy - https://goodnessofgodministries.international/2011/09/25/lionhearted-prayer-warriors-for-God-the-legendary-heroes-of-all-generations/

Samuel Chadwick said, "Nothing would turn the nation back to God so surely and so quickly as a Church that prayed and prevailed. The world will never believe in a religion in which there is no supernatural power. A rationalized faith, a socialized Church, and a moralized gospel may gain applause, but they awaken no conviction and win no converts."[2] Chadwick's statement sums up the dilemma we are facing as a church and perfectly describes what is happening, but it also gives the anecdote: a praying church that displays the supernatural.

A DIFFERENT TYPE OF DEMON SO WE HAVE TO PRAY DIFFERENTLY

There are different levels of prayer. The soft gentle approach to prayer that many of us are accustomed to or learned as a child will not be enough to confront the agenda of darkness in this last hour. That type of prayer is simply not enough to loosen the grip that satan has on our culture, churches, and families. The times we are living in are much different, but the good news is that satan's agenda can be stopped.

---

[2] Shorter, Kevin W. Shorter. *Prayer Quotes: Inspiration to Draw You Closer to God* . Kindle Edition.

There is a distinct type of prayer that is needed to neutralize satan's efforts and even drive him out. It is called fervent prayer.

When is the last time we approached prayer with a fire in our belly about an issue and/or the cause of Christ? Let me probe a little deeper. How intense is your prayer time? Is it methodical, boring, non-intrusive, predictable, lacking fire? This goes for our corporate prayer meetings as well. How intense is the corporate prayer time at your church? It doesn't mean there has to be a lot of yelling and screaming, but you can tell when people are interfacing with the Lord regarding the will of God for their lives and area.

This cannot be dismissed.

CHAOS AT THE BOTTOM OF THE MOUNTAIN

In Matthew 17, Jesus is with three of His closest friends: Peter, James, and John. They are on top of a mountain praying while the remaining disciples are at the foot of the mountain. Meanwhile, a desperate father brings his son, who is possessed by an evil spirit, to the disciples. This demon is ruthless and seeks the destruction and death of the child. The demons tried to drown the child and even tried to burn him alive (Matthew 17:15).

In Jesus' absence, the disciples tried to exorcise the demons out of the boy, but the text reveals **"...but they could not."** (Matthew 17:16). This means the demons defeated the disciples. I am certain the men were moved by this boy's condition and gave their best effort. The text, though, reveals that they failed. The nine disciples of Jesus lost this spiritual battle. Regardless of what they tried- technique, slogans, commands- none of it worked. It may have worked previously, but not this time. This time was different. Why? This demon was different.

The father didn't give up, for he knew that Jesus would eventually come down from the mountain. So he waited. And finally, when Jesus came down the father immediately brought his son to Jesus.

NOT HAPPY!

The Biblical text reveals that Jesus wasn't pleased with his disciples and their lack of results. In fact, Jesus rebuked them publicly (Matthew 17:17). Jesus was candid that He was disappointed in their inability to meet the need presented to them. After the Lord's chastisement, Jesus rebuked the tormenting spirits, and the young boy was gloriously set free.

Later that evening the disciples approached Jesus and asked Him a question. "Why couldn't we cast the demon out?" (Matthew 17:19). Pay close attention to Jesus' response...the answer will blow your mind...

So Jesus said to them, "Because of your unbelief; for assuredly, I say to you, if you have faith as a mustard seed, you will say to this mountain, 'Move from here to there,' and it will move; and nothing will be impossible for you.
21 However, **this kind** *does not go out except by prayer and fasting."*

Jesus spoke of the necessity of faith, and then He said something that described the type of battle the disciples were engaged in... Jesus said, **"THIS KIND."**

DON'T MISS THIS: The Greek word for **"this kind"** is génos which means, "this kindred, offspring, family, stock, lineage, breed, or nation." In other words, this *kind* of demon, this *type* of demon is different than the others.

Do you see it? This word implies that the devil inside that little boy was different than the other types of demons they were accustomed to confronting. It was stronger, more stubborn, more intense, and even more powerful than lower-level demons. Jesus, knowing this, sent a strong message to his followers that the only way to match and overcome this type of demon(s) is directly connected to prayer and fasting. Again, verse 21: "... **this kind** does not go out **except** by prayer and fasting."

There is no other option, no other alternative. Look again at what Jesus said, and let this fact sink in! He uses the word "except." He gives us the answer; He tells us that there is a way to defeat and to stop this type and lineage of devil. "FAST AND PRAY."

WHY IS THIS NECESSARY?

You and I will not have authority in the realm of the Spirit until we give ourselves to prayer. Jesus is stating emphatically that the authority to conquer in the spiritual realm is found in the secret place of prayer.

Fervent prayer and consistent fasting prepare us for the fierce battles ahead. These disciplines equip us and fine tuning our discernment, thus enabling our spirit man to operate without interference with the Spirit of God. In addition, fervent prayer and consistent fasting deafens the voice of the flesh, minimizes sin's appeal, and at the same time, compounds the voice of the Spirit in our heart. We become leaner and meaner in the Spirit realm. We actually increase our influence and history with God. Make no mistake about it- the devil knows the difference between those who fast and pray and those who do not. He knows who walks in Kingdom authority. For example, in Acts 19:15, the evil spirits in a demonized man spoke loudly to the would be exorcists, "…Jesus I know and Paul I know but who are you?" These demons were acutely aware that the ministry of the sons of Sceva posed no serious threat to their occupation and position of influence inside the man. They were safe and unafraid. However, the Apostle Paul was on their "watchlist," and they knew he had authority and power to remove them. This is why they said, *"Jesus I know, Paul I know, but who are you?"*

We can no longer choose to ignore our personal responsibility in the spiritual warfare of our age. We have to embrace the conflict and engage appropriately. People are depending on us. And dare I say, God is depending on us.

May the devil know you by name!

3

PREVAILING FERVENT PRAYER

"Oh! One hour with God infinitely exceeds all the pleasures and delights of this lower world."
David Brainerd
(1718–1747)

James 5:16 says, *"Confess your trespasses to one another, and pray for one another, that you may be healed. The effective, **fervent** prayer of a righteous man avails much."*

Exactly what is meant when the text says a "fervent prayer avails much?" *Webster's New World Dictionary of American English* gives us an idea what is implied by James. Webster's defines fervent as "hot; burning; glowing; having or showing great warmth of feeling; intensely devoted or earnest, ardent." This begs the question: "Does this describe my prayer life?"

For starters, we learn this kind of prayer is quite the opposite of a lethargic, cold, disconnected, or superficial type of praying. Fervent prayer is not mundane praying; fervent prayer is what I call **"warrior intercession."** Fervent prayer refuses to give up and is passionate, firm, constant, and intense. It fights until the answer comes. It stays in the battle for as long as it takes.

Prevailing fervent prayer is taking hold of God and not letting go. It is finding Him and refusing to relent. This is exactly what God wants us to do...

> *"... let him take hold of My strength...."*
> Isaiah 27:5

The literal Hebrew of Isaiah 27:5 is, *"Let them take hold of me."* It is a pressing into God and grasping Him. This is more than just a nonchalant approach to God in prayer. This is intentional intercession that latches onto God.

HERE IS WHAT HAPPENS WHEN WE DO THIS

There are two words that describe what effectual fervent prayer does. These words are "avails much." In the Greek this phrase means, **"granting great power for extraordinary deeds."** Again, this type of praying is different. And what I love about it is that it produces an advantage for the people of God. It allows the will of God to be enforced against the resistance of the enemy. It gets results. This is beautiful and should change our perspective of prayer.

I encourage you to memorize different versions of James 5:16 they translate *"avails much."*

> "...The earnest prayer of a righteous person has great power and produces **wonderful results**. (NLT)

> "...The prayer of a righteous man being made effective **prevails much**. (Berean Literal Bible)

> "...A prayer of a righteous person, when it is brought about, can **accomplish much**." (NASB)

> "...The earnest (heartfelt, continued) prayer of a righteous man makes **tremendous power available [dynamic in its working**) (AMPC)

This is absolute fire! It should make you want to pray right now!

TAKE A CLOSER LOOK

I want to draw your attention again to the Berean Literal Bible Translation - it says effectual fervent praying *"prevails much."* What does this mean? How does this work?

Are you ready for this? Are you sitting down? Here is the Oxford Dictionary definition of prevail - **"Prove more powerful than <u>opposing</u> forces; be <u>victorious</u>."**

READ THIS NEXT PART SLOWLY: This literally means that when we pray prevailing fervent prayers, we are increasing and releasing the power to prevail over every circumstance we face. Every demonic assignment can be matched and overwhelmed with the fulness of God's power. According to this extraordinary verse, our prayers are more powerful than ANY and ALL of the enemy's opposing forces. This also means when we pray fervently that God, on our behalf, discharges all the resources necessary to grant our requests. God literally dispatches angels, activates the necessary people, or moves the mountains Himself in order to accomplish His will! Our prayers do this! We are cooperating with God, and releasing His will on the earth.

Prayer was never intended for us to simply utter a few words heavenward and hoping something sticks. No! Prevailing fervent prayer is next dimension praying. It is intended to release the intervention and/or action of God on a situation to not only crush, but defeat the enemy.

GOING AGAINST THE STREAM

This kind of intensified prayer is clothed with the might of God. Cheerfully engage yourself in it. Don't be a spectator; be the initiator. However, be warned! This level of prayer will involve all aspects of your physical makeup. There are times you can be so engaged in this level of praying that you experience mental and physical exhaustion. You may feel depleted as you contended for the will of God to be done. Martin Luther understood the full weight that is carried by this type of intercession when he said, "Prayer is indeed a continuous violent action of the spirit as it is lifted up to God. This action is comparable to that of a ship going against the stream."[3]

Luther's words are interesting. I am sure he chose them carefully. He calls this type of intercession, **"violent action of the spirit."** Have you engaged in this type of prayer before? If not, can you see yourself taking "violent action of the spirit" while praying? Obviously, this may be new to you, but it is not foreign to the great moves of God.

---

[3] Donald G. Bloesch, *Struggle of Prayer* (Colorado Springs: Helmers and Howard, 1988), 132.

Embrace this level of warfare, don't ignore it or run from it. God will reward you as you release the forces necessary to triumph and advance the cause of the Kingdom of God.

Ask the Lord to teach you to pray this way.

4

THERE IS NO OTHER OPTION

"Work as if you were to live a hundred years,
Pray as if you were to die tomorrow."
Benjamin Franklin

Do you want to get results when you pray? We all do. Here is the secret: pray fervently!

Fervent prayer has been at the root of every significant move of God the world has ever seen. Fervent prayer changes history. It alters the now and secures a different future. At no time in recent history have we needed effectual, fervent prayers as we do now! This type of praying blasts the enemy's fortifications and prepares a platform for God to manifest His strength.

Remember Elijah? He prayed with emotion and a wild ferocious boldness. He was borderline reckless in his prayers. Once, he cried for fire to come down from heaven to consume the sacrifice on the altar - AND IT DID! Then he prayed it wouldn't rain - AND IT DIDN'T! Later he prayed for the rain to fall to end the drought - AND IT DID!

Fervent prayer has a certain flair to it. It is elegantly violent. It is humbling and yet fierce. Being in the presence of someone who prays this way can make you feel uncomfortable-not only with the intensity and focus of the prayer, but also, what they are requesting and demanding. If you are not prepared, this type of praying can catch you off guard. You will be challenged and convicted at the same time.

This type of fervent praying is beautiful and tenacious- persuasive and fiery at the same time. There is a simple confidence attached to it. It isn't arrogant, but is courageously calm with certainty that God is hearing and will respond. You can recognize when someone is fervently praying - it's hard to explain it, but you know when you hear it. You can feel it!

AGONIZING PLEADINGS

The late British Methodist minister William Booth, who founded the Salvation Army, knew something about fervent praying.

He once said,

> *"You must pray with your might... That does not mean saying your prayers, or*

sitting gazing about in church or chapel, with eyes wide open, while someone else says them for you. It means fervent, effectual, untiring wrestling with God. It means that grappling with Omnipotence, that clinging to Him, following Him about, so to speak, day and night, as the widow did to the unjust judge, with agonizing pleadings and arguments and entreaties, until the answer comes and the end is gained."

He added,

"This kind of prayer, be sure, the devil and the world and your own indolent, unbelieving nature will oppose. They will pour water on this flame. They will ply you with suggestions and difficulties. They will ask you how you can expect that the plans and purposes and feelings of God can be altered by your prayers. They will talk about impossibilities and predict failures; but, if you mean to succeed, you must shut your ears and eyes to all but what God has said, and hold Him to His own word: and you cannot do this in any sleepy mood; you cannot be a prevailing Israel unless you wrestle as Jacob wrestled, regardless of time aught else, save

obtaining the blessing sought—that is, you must pray with your might."[4]

These words by Booth are some of the most insightful and revelatory words regarding fervent prayer I have ever read. Those two previous paragraphs are a treasure trove of wisdom. In fact, in all of my research on this subject none capture the true spirit of what to expect when you participate in fervent praying. I would encourage you to read his statement again and again.

LOST PRAYERS

Not all praying is the same. Fervency in prayer cannot be attained without earnestness. Earnest praying is heartfelt praying that is accompanied with a compelling sense of urgency.

Julius W. Acker's writes in his book *Teach Us to Pray*, "Cold, lifeless, and idle prayers are like birds without wings ... mere lip prayers are lost prayers."[5]

Our prayers must have depth and weight. The issue(s) we take to the Father must matter to us.

---

[4] *God's Generals: The Revivalists*, Roberts Liardon, 2008

[5] J. W. Acker, *Teach Us to Pray* (St. Louis: Concordia, 1961), 31.33.

We can no longer afford to give our time and efforts to emotionless praying. Finney recognized that those who made great contributions to the kingdom of God through prayer all had something in common: they felt, "the pressure of a great cause."

Jesus was accustomed to fervent praying. We read in Hebrews 5:7 that *"during the days of Jesus' life on earth, he offered up prayers and petitions with loud cries and tears"*. Here is the same verse in the Amplified Version,

"In the days of His earthly life, Jesus offered up both [specific] petitions and [urgent] supplications [for that which He needed] with fervent crying and tears to the One who was [always] able to save Him from death, and He was heard because of His reverent submission toward God [His sinlessness and His unfailing determination to do the Father's will]."

I am thankful for this passage in Hebrews because it sheds light on how Jesus prayed. He was fully engaged to the "great cause" before Him. He prayed with great fervency and passion. And let us not forget that He is our prototype - the one we should emulate.

Richard Watson, a British Methodist theologian, wrote, "Prayer without fervency is no prayer; it is speaking, not praying. Lifeless prayer is no more prayer than a picture of a man is a man."

In his book, *The Essentials of Prayer*, author E.M. Bounds wrote, "Prayer must be aflame. Its ardor must consume. Prayer without fervor is as a sun without light or heat, or as a flower without beauty or fragrance.[6]

It is imperative that we capture the necessary components for Kingdom moving prayer. God's Word and His Prayer Generals throughout history know what successful prayer looks like, and we must glean from them. If we are going to pray, we must do it right way. Harold Lindsell wrote, "Prayer does not come naturally to men. It must be learned. Learning to pray...includes knowledge of the laws governing prayer as well as experience gained in the practice of prayer. Prayer must be nourished and cultivated if it is to grow."[7]

HEAVEN IS TOO BUSY

---

[6] E. M. Bounds on Prayer, E. M. Bounds, 1922

[7] Harold Lindsell, When You Pray (Grand Rapids: Baker Book House, 1969), 25–26.

Bounds commented again, "Heaven is too busy to listen to half-hearted prayers."[8] It is a fact that half-hearted prayers won't persevere when there is demonic resistance or a prolonged delay. Furthermore, dull praying will not prevail against the spirit of infirmity or cancel the assignment of the enemy on your family. It takes more, much more. A passionless prayer is no threat to satan and his work. It is easy to go through the motions and half-heartedly pray. We must resist the lure of saying a few words and calling it prayer. Plus, we can no longer casually attend corporate prayer meetings. We need the attitude of "I have come to fight in the spirit for revival. I have come to fight for my loved ones and for the Kingdom of God to become a reality in our church."

A CHANCE TO CHANGE HISTORY

Please do not take lightly the ministry of prayer. It is one of the highest callings within the body of Christ. We need everyone in the body of Christ to run to it and fully embrace it. It will change your world, literally. When discussing prevailing fervent prayer, Samuel Chadwick commented, "It prevails. It turns ordinary mortals into men of power. It brings power. It brings fire. It brings rain. It brings life. It brings God. There is no

---

[8] E.M. Bounds, *Purpose in Prayer,* 59.

power like that of prevailing prayer."[9] He adds, "Intensity is a law of prayer...wrestling prayer prevails. The fervent, effectual prayer of the righteous is of great force... We must never try to work up an emotion of intensity... If the spirit groans in intercession, do not be afraid of the agony of prayer. There are blessings of the kingdom that are only yielded to the violence of the vehement soul."[10]

[9] Samuel Chadwick, *Path of Prayer*, (Kansas City: Beacon Press, 1931), 81–82.

[10] Ibid., 68.

5

"YOU PRAY OVER THERE, WE WILL PRAY HERE"

"History is silent about revivals that did not begin with prayer."
Edwin Orr

Prevailing prayer creates a dynamic culture of unfathomable conviction not only in the local church but the community as a whole. The net effect: people who were closed to the gospel suddenly become awakened to the barrenness of their soul, their sins, and their need to make peace with God as soon as possible.

Like many of you I love to study revivals and great moves of God. The Hebrides Revival (1949-1953) is my favorite of all the past revivals.

The most significant minister in this revival was the evangelist, Duncan Campbell. Via invitation, he went to the Isle of Lewis to conduct a two-week evangelistic campaign; however, due to the revival, he remained on the Island for two years.

After the revival was over, Campbell had the opportunity to describe how the revival started, plus explain some of the high points of this extraordinary move of God. I find his assessment fascinating.

Here are is his exact words.

> "First, I would like to make it perfectly clear that I did not bring revival to the Hebrides. It has grieved me beyond words to hear people talk and write about 'the man who brought revival to the Hebrides.' My dear people, I didn't do that. The revival was there before I ever set foot on the island. It began in a gracious awareness of God sweeping through the parish of Barvas."

> He added, "In November 1949, this gracious movement began on the island of Lewis. Two old women (Peggy and Christine Smith), one of them 84 years of age and the other 82 (one of them stone blind), were greatly burdened because of the appalling state of their own parish. It was true that not a single young person

attended public worship. Not a single young man or young woman went to the church.

One night one of the sisters had a vision. Now, remember, in revival God works in wonderful ways. A vision came to one of them, and in the vision, she saw the church of her fathers crowded with young people, packed to the doors, and a strange minister, standing in the pulpit. She was so impressed by the vision that she sent for the parish minister. And of course, he, knowing the two sisters, knowing that they were two women who knew God in a wonderful way, responded to their invitation and called at the cottage. That morning one of the sisters said to the minister, "You must do something about this. And I would suggest that you call your elders together and that you spend at least two nights with us in prayer a week, Tuesday and Friday. If you gather your elders together, you can meet in a barn or a farming community, and **as you pray there, we will pray here.**" Well, that was what happened; the minister called his elders together, and seven of them met in a barn to pray on Tuesday and on Friday. And the two old women got on their knees and prayed with them.

That continued for some weeks, in fact, I believe almost a month and a half. Then, one night as they were kneeling there in the barn and pleading this promise, "*I will pour water on him that is thirsty, and floods upon the dry ground*," a certain young man, a deacon in the church, got up and read Psalm 24: "*Who shall ascend into the hill of the Lord? Or who shall stand in his holy place? He that hath clean hands, and a pure heart; who hath not lifted up his soul unto vanity, nor sworn deceitfully. He shall receive the blessing [not a blessing, but the blessing] from the Lord*" (vv.3-5a). And then that young man closed his Bible. And looking down at the minister and the elders, he spoke these crude words, "It seems to me to be so much humbug to be praying as we are praying, to be waiting as we are waiting, if we ourselves are not rightly related to God." And then he lifted his two hands and prayed, "God, are my hands clean? Is my heart pure?"[11]

Campbell continues, "But he got no further. That young man fell to his knees and then fell into a trance. Now don't ask

[11] https://thecomingrevival.com/duncan-campbell-on-lewis-revival/

me to explain this because I can't. He fell into a trance and was now lying on the floor of the barn. And in the words of the minister, at that moment he and the other ministers were gripped by the conviction that a God-sent revival must ever be related to holiness and godliness. Are my hands clean? Is my heart pure? This is the man whom God will trust with revival; that was the conviction.

When that happened in the barn, the power of God swept into the parish. And an awareness of God gripped the community such as had not been known for over a hundred years. An awareness of God—that's revival! And on the following day, the looms were silent, and little work was done on the farms as men and women gave themselves to thinking about eternal things, gripped by eternal realities.

I shall never forget the night that I arrived at the piers in the mail steamer. I was standing in the presence of the minister whom I had never seen, and two of his elders that I never knew. The minister turned to me and said: "Mr. Campbell, I know that you are very tired. You have been travelling all day by train, to begin with, and then by steamer. And I am sure that you are ready for your supper and ready for your bed. But I wonder if you would be prepared to address a meeting in the parish church at nine o'clock tonight on our way home. It will be a short meeting, and then we will make for the manse, and you will get your supper and your bed, and rest until tomorrow evening." Well, it will interest you to know that I never got that supper.

We got to the church about a quarter to nine to find about three hundred people gathered. I gave an address. Nothing really happened during the service. It was a good meeting. There was a sense of God and a consciousness of His Spirit moving, but nothing beyond that. So I pronounced the benediction, and we were leaving the church around a quarter to eleven.

Just as I was walking down the aisle along with this young deacon who had read the Psalm in the barn, he suddenly stood in the aisle and, looking up to the heavens said: "God, You can't fail us! God, You can't fail us! You promised to pour water on the thirsty and floods upon the dry ground. God, You can't fail us!"

Soon he was on his knees in the aisle praying, and then he fell into a trance once again. Just then, the door opened. It was then eleven o'clock. The door of the church opened, and the local blacksmith came back into the church and said, "Mr. Campbell, something wonderful has happened. Oh, we were praying that God would pour water on the thirsty and floods upon the dry ground, and listen, He's done it! He's done it!"

When I went to the door of the church, I saw a congregation of approximately six hundred people. Where had they come from? What had happened? I believe that very night God swept by in Pentecostal power, the power of the Holy Ghost. And what happened in the early days of the Apostles was now happening in the parish of Barvas.

Over a hundred young people were at the dance in the parish hall, and they weren't thinking of God or eternity. They were there to have a good night when suddenly the power of God fell upon the dance. The music ceased, and in a matter of minutes, the hall was empty.

Over a hundred young people were at the dance in the parish hall, and they weren't thinking of God or eternity. God was not in any of their thoughts. They were there to have a good night when suddenly the power of God fell upon the dance. The music ceased, and in a matter of minutes, the hall was empty. They fled from the hall as a man fleeing from a plague, and they made for the church. They were standing outside, and they saw lights in the church, and that it was a house of God, so they went in.

Men and women who had gone to bed rose, dressed, and made for the church. There had been nothing done in the way of publicity, no mention of a special effort, except an announcement from the pulpit on the Sabbath that a certain man was going to be conducting a series of meetings in the parish covering ten days. But God took the situation in hand. Oh, He became His own publicity agent. A hunger and a thirst gripped the people. Six hundred of them were now at the church standing outside.

I found a young woman, a teacher in the grammar school, lying prostrate on the floor of the pulpit praying, "Oh, God, is there mercy for me? Oh, God, is there mercy for me?" She was one of those at the dance. But she was now lying on the floor of the pulpit crying to God for mercy.

As I was leaving the church, a young man came to me and said, "Mr. Campbell, I would like you to go to the police station."

I said, "The police station? What's wrong?"

"Oh," he said, "There's nothing wrong, but there must be at least four hundred people gathered around there just now."

Now the sergeant there was a God-fearing man. He was in the meeting. And next to the police station was the cottage in which the two old women lived. People knew that this was a home that feared God. I believe that that had something to do with the magnet, the power that drew men."

God saturated the Hebrides, and He seemed to be everywhere. People came to the Lord by the thousands because two ladies prayed. Oh, may we never underestimate the impact our prayers make on our culture, on our community, and on the people we love.

God, raise up another set of women like Peggy and Christine!

PEGGY AND CHRISTINE

These sisters, Peggy and Christine, were the catalyst of a world-shaking revival. In the natural, these ladies were nothing special. In fact, they were most common and simple. In the world's standard, they were just ordinary. Not only were they advanced in years, each had debilitating physical issues. Again, Peggy, 84 years old, was completely blind, and her sister Christine, 82 years old, was bent over with arthritis. However, these ladies cried out to God, and God responded!

Can this happen again?

LET'S DO THE MATH

Think about it, what would happen if took their advice:

"YOU PRAY THERE, WE WILL PRAY OVER HERE!"

Currently in North America, there are approximately 400,000 churches that meet each week. They come to worship and to hear the Word of God preached. What do you think would happen if once a week each church conducted a prayer meeting for the sole purpose of praying for revival?

Let's do the math. Let's assume on average 30 people gather to pray at each church. If that happened, then **12,000,000** Christians would come together each week seeking the face of God for revival.

12 MILLION

I can hear people asking, "Is this really necessary?" Or, they think, "Isn't it enough for just a handful of people to pray? Won't God respond to them?" Well, my answer is this: more is always better! Hundreds praying are better than dozens; thousands are better than hundreds, and millions are better than thousands. Right now, we have a trickle, and we need a river! We need more intercessors!

If millions of people gathered for the sole purpose of seeing God in prayer, what do you think would be the result? God would come! Revival would come! An awakening would come! Our churches would change, our homes would be blessed, our communities would improve, and the local schools would be impacted. Our nation would turn to God.

Dear friend, this is a clarion call for each of us. If we don't answer the call to prayer things will only get worse…things will not work themselves out. No, our society will only drift further and further from God.

Pastor, (or whoever can), start a corporate prayer time. If you already have a corporate prayer time in place, promote it above everything else in the church. Prayer is the most important thing we do. And remember, **"AS YOU PRAY THERE, WE WILL PRAY OVER HERE."**

6

IT WAS JUST ANOTHER SERMON UNTIL...

*"Whenever God is preparing to do
something great in the earth,
He first sets His people a-praying!"*
Matthew Henry

In this chapter, I want to share several examples how prayer changes sermons, preachers, and entire meetings. My prayer is that each of us understand that prayer is the mightiest force in the world; it has no equal. It is boundless, and when applied, it accomplishes all that God desires.

Jonathan Edwards summoned a group of his followers at Enfield, Connecticut with one goal - seeking God for a powerful move of the Holy

Spirit to accompany their work. Their burden lead Edwards and the team to pray all night one Saturday evening.[12]

While the adjacent cities and towns were receptive to the work of the Holy Spirit and experiencing a touch from heaven, the city of Enfield was not. It was becoming notorious for resisting the work of God at the time. However, all this changed when a group of people gathered together and prayed throughout the night. They interceded for God to move upon the meeting and for God to move on the word being preached. The next day Edward's sermon, *"Sinners in the Hands of an Angry God"* was greatly anointed by the Holy Spirit.

In the middle of his sermon, many in the congregation were clinging to the pillars of the church, moaning extensively. Deep groans could be heard throughout the building. They literally felt they were slipping into hell. Some cried out while Edwards was preaching, "Oh, I am going to Hell—Oh, what shall I do for Christ?"

As Edwards continued his message, others felt the fire of God on them. Many fell to the floor in agony; they shrieked and cried out. The crying and weeping became so loud that Edwards was forced to discontinue the sermon.

---

[12] S. B. Shaw, Touching Incidents and Remarkable Answers to Prayer (Chicago: S. B. Shaw, n.d.), 153.

God's convicting power was overwhelming to all in the room. It was unbearable. What made the difference? The all-night prayer meeting shifted the atmosphere and set Edward's message on fire. After this powerful service and demonstration of the efficacy of prayer, Edwards stepped forward and instructed Christians to join in meetings of united prayer across New England until God visited them all with revival.

AN UNNAMED CRIPPLED MAN

George Whitefield, who many called the greatest preacher of all time, was used by God to shake America and the British Isles in the mid 1700's. His ministry fanned the flames of revival throughout the world, especially during the Great Awakening. There are many factors that helped fashion and mold Whitefield's public ministry. However, not many people are aware that as he traveled, a prayer partner went with him. This man was crippled, but he knew how to pray. Glen Clark said, "His prayers, even more than Whitefield's preaching, were the cause of the wonderful results."[13]

---

[13] Frank C. Laubach, *Prayer* (Westwood, N.J.: Revell, 1946), 30.

God will take anyone who is willing to give themselves to prayer and become a part of His ever-increasing hidden army. Personally, it is the perfect opportunity to make a forceful contribution to the work of God on the earth. As mentioned above, the unnamed crippled man who thrived behind the scenes was just as important, if not more so, than Whitefield's public ministry.

FIRE IN THE ENGINE

E.M Bounds gave this insight on why prayer is a necessity.

"As the engine never moves until the fire is kindled, so preaching, with all its machinery, perfection, and polish is at a dead standstill as far as spiritual results are concerned, till prayer has kindled and created the steam. The texture, fineness, and strength of the sermon is as so much rubbish unless the might impulse of prayer is in it, through it, and behind it. The preacher must, by prayer put God in the sermon. The preacher must, by prayer move God toward the people, before he can move the people to God by his words. The preacher must have had audience and ready access to God before he can have access to the people."[14]

SLIPPING INTO HELL

The Irish revival of 1859, also known as the "Ulster Revival," began in late 1857 when a young man named James McQuilkin, and a few others started holding weekly prayer meetings in the schoolhouse near Kells, County Antrim. They prayed for nearly two years, and their unwavering commitment to seek God sparked a move of God in towns like Ahoghill and Ballymena. It is reported that the glory of God was so strong in some of the meetings that people became so weak they could not get back to their homes. Men and women would fall by the wayside and would be found hours later pleading with God to save their souls. They felt as if they were slipping into hell, and that nothing else in life mattered but to get right with God. To them eternity meant everything. Nothing else was of any consequence. They felt that if God did not have mercy on them and save them, they were doomed for all time to come.

The Irish Revival was birthed when people gathered together to pray. Never forget, the moment you begin to pray you are fighting for God on the earth!

---

[14] E.M. Bounds, *A Treasury of Prayer*, (Offspring Publishers, Siloam Springs, AR, pp.93-94)

THE ATMOSPHERE WAS DEAD

Dwight L. Moody, in one of his evangelistic campaigns, visited Oxford and Cambridge Universities. The atmosphere was anything but receptive to the message of the cross. The students in adjacent spaces were so rowdy it was difficult for hear the words coming forth from the pulpit. Moody had enough and summoned three hundred women of Cambridge to meet in Alexander Hall for a period of intercession. The ladies prayed for the kids to fall under conviction and meet God. That very evening, the atmosphere shifted. Multiple students repented of their sins and became born again. Moody commented that this was the greatest victory of his life.[15]

What made the difference? What changed the atmosphere for Moody? What was the catalyst for this move of God? Prayer.

THIS IS FOR YOU...

You are a change agent! You may think you are unimportant and insignificant. This is completely untrue. I have a few words of encouragement for you.

---

[15] Arthur T. Pierson, *The Miracles of Missions* (New York: Funk & Wagnalls, 1901), 21–22.

-You may struggle with sharing your faith; you may fail more than you succeed, **but you can pray**.

-You may coward in fear when asked to speak publicly, **but you can pray**.

-You may not be able to sing, **but you can pray.**

-If your cry is for God to use you...**start here - pray**.

Prayer is where He needs you the most. Prayer is not popular. You may not receive public recognition for praying, but one day when you stand before the King at the Judgment Seat of Christ, He will reveal to you and to the whole world how mighty you were on your knees. Right now, if you pray, your earthly influence will be incalculable,

Will you be like Edwards prayer team or the crippled man who prayed so the work of God could go forth in power? Can God count on you to be in his hidden army of prayer warriors?

7

A JESUS MAN IS COMING

"The devil is not terribly frightened of our human efforts and credentials. But he knows his kingdom will be damaged when we begin to lift up our hearts to God.
Jim Cymbala

The day is upon us when more and more people in the body of Christ are living and walking in an usual amount of God's glory. I am actually noticing this as I travel and minister. The glory of the Most High is covering them like a blanket.

The enemy is keenly aware of those who are mere pretenders and professors of God's power from those who actually possess the anointing of the Holy Spirit. Rest assured satan has marked those who render a threat to his territorial dominion. His eyes are ever observing their activity as he guards and moves to protect his treasure.

THE DEVIL ASKED, "WHO ARE YOU?"

In Acts 19, one of the greatest stories of the New Testament is told. In fact, it is not only serious for all the right reasons, but I must admit it is seriously funny as well.

A group of Jewish exorcists confidently approached a demonized man and attempted to cast out the devil. They addressed the devil and commanded it to come in Jesus' name. However, to their surprise the devil spoke back. The demon made it clear that he wasn't going anywhere because he didn't recognize them as anointed followers of Christ. The demon said, "Jesus I know, Paul I know, **but who are you?**" (Acts 19:15)

These exorcists were openly rebuked by a demon. If that wasn't bad enough, the Bible tell us that the devil leaped on the men, beating them so badly that they fled the scene completely naked and wounded. (v.16) Wow, talk about a bad day.

This remarkable episode reveals to us that the devil and his demons are aware of when someone is an actual threat to them. There are different dimensions of power and authority in Christianity, and those who pray fervently fit into the classification of being a threat to the devil. Why? Because they are submitting their lives to

Kingdom purpose. Most importantly, prevailing fervent prayers dislodge satan's legal right to be somewhere, and he simply doesn't like it.

DO IT AGAIN LORD!

This story below is riveting and allows us to peek into the inner workings of the demonic realm. Do not think for a moment that the devil isn't aware of who prays and of the individuals who carry God's weight and power.

A Chinese Christian boy of twelve years of age, named Ma-Na-Si, left boarding school and came home for a vacation time. As he stood on the doorstep of his father's home, he heard a horseman galloping up to him. The man, a non-Christian, was greatly agitated and wanted to see the Jesus man—the pastor, the boy's father—immediately. Ma-Na-Si explained that his father was away from home. The visitor became very distressed. He said he had been sent to get the Jesus man to cast a demon out of a young woman in his village. She was torn by demons, raving, reviling, pulling out her hair, clawing her face, tearing her clothes, smashing up furniture, and dashing down food dishes. He described her blasphemy, her raging outbursts, and her foaming at the mouth until she was exhausted physically and mentally.

The boy kept explaining, "But my father is not here. My father is not here." Finally, the frenzied man fell on his knees and said, "You, too, are a Jesus man. Will you come?" The boy was surprised for a moment. Then he made himself available to Jesus. Like little Samuel, he was willing to obey God in everything. He agreed to go with the stranger, who then jumped on his horse and put the boy behind him. As they galloped away, Ma-Na-Si began to pray. He had accepted an invitation to cast out a demon in the name of Jesus, but was he worthy to be used by God? He searched his heart, prayed for guidance, what to say and how to act. He tried to remember how Jesus had dealt with the demons. Then he simply trusted God's power and mercy and asked for Jesus to be glorified.

When they arrived at the house, several family members were by force holding the tortured woman upon the bed. She had not been told that someone had gone for the pastor. But when she heard footsteps outside, she called out, "All of you get out of my way quickly, so that I can escape. I must flee! A Jesus man is coming. I cannot endure him. His name is Ma-Na-Si."

Ma-Na-Si entered the room. He sang a Christian song, praising the Lord Jesus, and in the name of Jesus Christ, the risen Lord, glorified, and omnipotent, he commanded the demon to come out of the woman. Instantly she was calm. From that day on, she was perfectly well. She was amazed when they told her that she had announced the name of the Christian boy who was coming. Even a twelve-year-old by Christ's authority can bind Satan's demon and cast him out.[16]

PARALYZED BY PRAYER

This is what prevailing fervent prayer accomplishes. You become a mighty force on the earth and subsequently, known throughout the sulphury regions of hell. Praying people are the most feared people group in hell. Demons despise intercessors. Oswald Chambers accurately captured this sentiment, "The prayer of the feeblest saint who lives in the Spirit and keeps right with God is a terror to Satan. The very powers of darkness are paralyzed by prayer; no spiritualistic séance can succeed in the

---

[16] Unknown Christian, *Kneeling Christian*, (Christian Classics Ethereal Library, Grand Rapids, MI) 102–104.

presence of a humble praying saint. No wonder Satan tries to keep our minds fussy in active work till we cannot think in prayer."

Let us remember what the Wesleyan Methodist minister Samuel Chadwick said, "The one concern of the devil is to keep the saints from praying. He fears nothing from prayerless studies/work/Christian activities. He laughs at our toil, mocks our wisdom but trembles when we pray."

We cannot be unclear about this fact: your prayers methodically and devastatingly advance the kingdom of God. Your prayers actually render the powers of the demonic realm ineffective. The devil has no option but to give up gained ground and retreat.

This is why the devil's chief concern is to keep us from praying. It was Andrew Boner that said, "The prince of the power of the air seems to bend all the force of his attack against the spirit of prayer."

Stay low and keep praying!

8

HE DIED TOO YOUNG

"God shapes the world by prayer."
E.M. Bounds

On a muggy afternoon I found myself on South Main Street traveling to the grave site of a 37-year-old who died in the prime of his life. I slowly made the turn into Adams Rural Cemetery located in Adams, New York. As the car slowly rolled to a stop, I hesitated before exiting the car knowing I was about to be at the grave of one of the Lord's greatest intercessors who ever lived. I took a deep breath and opened the door; the moment was sacred, so I remained quiet. As I began to walk toward the cemetery plot, each step was carefully measured as my heart rate increased. After a few minutes, I found the head marker where I reverently stood in silence at the foot of the grave of Abel Clary. The moment was surreal, heavy, demanding, intimidating, and inspiring. I just stood there, saying nothing, just looking and listening to the silence. I was swept up in the moment and looking to the Father to teach me all I could learn in this moment.

Even though Abel Clary only lived 37 years, his life had a major influence on the great Charles Finney and on the entire body of Christ. In fact, because this young man understood the power of prayer, the impact his life made then is still being felt today.

WHAT IS THE CONNECTION?

We know that Clary was good friends with Daniel Nash. Nash received notoriety because he was the lead intercessor for Charles Finney. Clary felt God leading him to unite with Father Nash and join him to pray for Charles Finney.

This is how author Steve Porter explains their efforts, "Nash and Clary would quietly enter a town before services even began, rent whatever space they could afford, enlist the help of other like-minded believers, and gather to pray for endless hours, covering the upcoming evangelistic services. They fasted and prayed before, during and after the services ended, for Heaven to open and the Holy Spirit's presence to invade Earth as never before, bringing men to their knees in humble repentance. They were desperate for souls to be saved from eternal hell, and their fervent prayers actually birthed a great awakening that, in the end, turned their world upside down. On their knees, they prayed until the damp, dark prayer cellars were aflame with the very fire of the Holy Spirit."[17]

Clary very rarely, if ever, demanded attention and was very seldom seen in public. He literally gave himself to not just praying, but to revival praying. There is a notable difference between the two. Clary prayed incessantly for Finney and did not stop praying until the crusade(s) were over. He pleaded for the Kingdom of God to come and fall upon all who were at the meeting and beyond. History accurately reveals that this was the secret to Finney's success.

Charles Finney loved Abel Clary. He described Clary this way:

> "He had been licensed to preach; but his spirit of prayer was such, he was so burdened with the souls of men, that he was not able to preach much, his whole time and strength being given to prayer. The burden of his soul would frequently be so great that he was unable to stand, and he would writhe and groan in agony. I was well acquainted with him, and knew

---

[17] https://static1.squarespace.com/static/
54791966e4b0306d2b1b6002/t/
5d8252689cc746608830b8d2/1568821865080/
Final+Abel+B+Clary+Article_+Steve+Porter.pdf

---

something of the wonderful spirit of prayer that was upon him. He was a very silent man, as almost all are who have that powerful spirit of prayer."

Finney adds, "The first I knew of his being in Rochester, (New York) a gentleman who lived about a mile west of the city, called on me one day and asked me if I knew a Mr. Abel Clary, a minister. I told him that I knew him well. 'Well,' he said, 'he is at my house, and has been there for some time, and I don't know what to think of him.' I said, 'I have not seen him at any of our meetings.' 'No,' he replied, 'he cannot go to meeting, he says. He prays nearly all the time, day and night, and in such agony of mind that I do not know what to make of it. Sometimes he cannot even stand on his knees, but will lie prostrate on the floor, and groan and pray in a manner that quite astonishes me.' I said to the brother, 'I understand it: please keep still. It will all come out right; he will surely prevail. '"[18]

Finney said about Clary's tenacious spirit of prayer, "Mr. Clary continued as long as I did and did not leave until after I had left. He never

[18] https://ccel.org/ccel/torrey/pray/pray.i_1.xv.html

appeared in public, but gave himself wholly to prayer."

After Clary's death in 1833 Finney discovered Clary's journal. The secret pages highlighted the waves of burdens that Clary would carry in prayer. In fact, many of the moves of God Finney experienced during his meetings were directly connected to the exact time the burdens and sequences of prayer that Carey offered before the Lord.

Finney wrote in his personal journal about an event that occurred at a church and later in the home he visited.

> "One evening when preaching he recognized Abel Clary in a meeting and noticed that he seemed to be heavily burdened to pray, right then and there. Finney, who was well aware of the man's reputation as a powerful prayer warrior, was glad to have him there. His brother, Dr. Clary, was also a professor of religion but had none of his brother's gift for prayer. During a break between services, the doctor invited Finney to join them for lunch and a time of rest. Once they arrived at the house, it wasn't long before they were called to come and eat. Dr. Clary turned to his brother Abel and asked him to bless the food, and he nodded that he would.

However, he had scarcely spoken a word when he broke down, pushed his chair away from the table and fled to his room. The doctor, who assumed he was feeling ill, followed him, only to return a moment later, telling Finney that Abel wanted to see him.

When Finney asked what was wrong, he answered that he didn't know but that his brother appeared to be in great distress. He went on to say that he thought it was his state of mind that upset him so deeply.

When Finney arrived at his room, Clary lay groaning on his bed, and the evangelist realized that he was seeing evidence of the Spirit making intercession for him, with groanings that couldn't be uttered, exactly as described in Scripture. (Rom. 8:26)

Momentarily, Clary could scarcely speak when he said, "Pray, Brother Finney." Finney knelt beside his bed and prayed in English for the souls of the lost and continued to pray until Clary's distress passed as he lay there, utterly exhausted and spent.

Then Finney joined those at the table, amazed by what had happened. He knew that he had witnessed the voice of God, praying through Abel Clary, and he was convinced that God would use it in a powerful way. And that's exactly what happened. The pastor of the church hosting the revival later reported that over the six weeks he was preaching, 500 people had come to know the Lord."[19]

It is true that Abel Clary earned his place in revival history. Even though he died at such a young age, his prayer legacy lives on. May our hearts learn from his example.

Right now, ask the Lord to baptize you with the same spirit of prayer that Abel Clary had. Ask again and again and again until you are given to prayer. Heaven is willing to bestow this upon you. Ask until you receive!

---

[19] Hansen, Gary Neal. Kneeling with Giants (p. 4). InterVarsity Press. Kindle Edition.

9

THE DAY GOD WONDERED

"A man is what he is on his knees before God, and nothing more."
Robert M'Cheyne

"He saw that there was no man, And wondered that there was no intercessor…" Isaiah 59:16

One day it dawned on a minister the power of prayer can have on a society. "Man," he explained, "if this is true at all, it is the mightiest truth in the universe! It means that enough of us praying often enough could make everybody in the whole world look up and listen to God. We could transform the world."

Isaiah 59 tells us that God's people had been badly defeated by the Babylonians and their place of worship, the temple, had been destroyed. To make matters worse, God's people were taken away in chains from their land of promise. The situation was bleak and the people of God were in disarray. God knows the power of intercession, and Isaiah 59:16 reveals that God was trying to understand why there was no intercessor in Israel.

The New International Version of the Bible translates Isaiah 59:16 this way, "He saw that there was no one, he was **appalled**…"

The word appalled means "***devastated, displeased, astonished***."

The Berean Study Bible says, "He (God) was **amazed** that there was no one to intercede."

GOD WAS DISGUSTED

In short, God was in need of someone in Israel to rise up and to pray; however, no one did. Not only did their inaction puzzle God, but He was also astonished. The Contemporary English version of the Bible said, "It **disgusted**" God when no one came forward. Disgusted is a strong word to use to describe how God felt. The true essence of the word means there is a strong disapproval of an action or inaction.   It also means that one is outraged and very unhappy over what occurred or didn't occur.

Seeing how God responded to a prayerless Israel, I am left to wonder what God thinks about America today and His contemporary Church. We, too, are in crisis. Our nation has drifted from Him and is experiencing the full onslaught of attack from the enemy. Evil seems to be unopposed and spreading. In fact, things seem to be getting worse by the day. At the same time, far too many local churches are lukewarm and, for the most part, have proven to be ineffective at dispelling the darkness.

One has to consider: Is God wondering who will intercede for America? Who will man the wall to be a watchman for the cause of Christ? Will anyone embrace the arduous climb to the mountain of solitude to be alone with God? What pastor will reprioritize his agenda to make prayer the number one ministry of the church? What church will step forward and lead the way? Who among us will boldly stand in the gap between the living and the dead? Who will have the courage to take the horns of the altar and not let go until the fire of God falls? Is there someone, anyone, that will accept the challenge and wear the mantle of prayer warrior? Is there a Holy Rebel among the readers that will say "yes" to the dark closet, the place of isolation and separateness?

ISAIAH WANTED TO KNOW...

Later in Isaiah 64 the great Prophet wanted to know why **"NO ONE CALLS ON YOU or...stir themselves to take hold of God."** (Isaiah 64:7)

The Good News Translation puts it this way, "No one turns to you in prayer; no one goes to you for help...."

The word "stir" in the text means to "awaken" or "rise up." This expresses more than just going through the motions of prayer; it is earnest, heartfelt, intense, "effectual fervent" prayer. Isaiah wondered, given the nation's situation, why no one was arousing themselves to prayer.

Is this interesting? Paul said the same thing in Romans 13:11,

*"Do this, knowing that this is a critical time. It is already the hour for you to **awaken from your sleep** [of spiritual complacency]; for our salvation is nearer to us now than when we first believed [in Christ]."*

The scriptures are clear on this one thing. God is waiting on us to awaken ourselves and to take hold of Him. This is what He desires. If we do, He will respond.

"If My people who are called by My name will humble themselves, and pray and seek My face, and turn from their wicked ways,

*then I will hear from heaven, and will
forgive their sin and heal their land."*
2 Chronicles 7:14

I truly believe we all have a longing for true revival. Our conversations speak of revival. We point toward revival as what is necessary. We know revival is our only hope. But with that being said, does our prayer effort equal the desire?

Who will take hold of God? Who will seek Him until He comes? Who will pray until God responds?

E. M. Bounds declared, "Prayer is the contact of a living soul with God. In prayer, God stoops to kiss man, to bless man, and to aid in everything that God can devise or man can need."[20]

---

[20] E. M Bounds, The Necessity of Prayer, quoted in A Treasury of Prayer, compiled by Leonard Ravenhill (Minneapolis: Bethany Fellowship, 1961), 30.

10

THE WALL!

"If you don't want the devil to hit you, hit him first, and hit him with all your might, so that he may be too crippled to hit back."
C.T. Studd

The most famous wall in the world is the great wall of China. This massive structure stretches more than 13,000 miles and took over 2,300 years to build (680 BC–1681 AD). It literally took nine continuous dynasties to complete. This majestic wall methodically weaves its way through every possible terrain - deserts, mountains, plains, and plateaus. In the wall's conception, the primary function was clear. The wall was to be used as a defense mechanism to keep nomadic people away and to deter advancing armies.

In the ancient world of the Bible, cities had walls. These fortified cities gave the inhabitants a safe place to live in order to raise a family and to do commerce. Soldiers and protectants would be placed on top of the walls to watch for any potential threat. The inhabitants could carry on with their life during the day and could rest well at night knowing they were protected if aggressors chose to attack.

LOOKING FOR A BREACH IN THE WALL

If a breach or gap in the wall was left unattended or in disrepair, the city would be highly vulnerable and unable to adequately repel an advancing army. Naturally, the invaders would capitalize on the breach and send troops to advance forcefully through the opening in order to conquer the city. Unattended breaches are not only problematic but also dangerous to any walled civilization.

In Ezekiel 22, God highlights how wicked His people became. The nation at every level had completely abandoned God. Obviously, this was not pleasing to the Lord, and after years of wooing and pursuing His people, God had no other alternative but to bring forth His judgment.

However, even in the midst of all the rebellion God was looking for a way to spare His people from the wrath to come - Ezekiel 22:30.

"So I sought for a man among them who would make a wall, and stand in the gap before Me on behalf of the land, that I should not destroy it; but I found no one."

God was looking for someone to stand before Him to plead the case of the people. He needed an intercessor, someone who would cry out for God's mercy. The text reveals that God **"SOUGHT FOR A MAN** who would stand before Me."

The posture of God's heart was to spare the people to postpone His judgment, to delay His wrath; however, no one responded. Not one person stepped up and said, "Hey, we have a problem and God is not pleased with us. Perhaps we need to pray."

I am sure it is safe to assume that the overall sentiment among the people was that someone else would certainly come forward and take care of this. In other words, a well-qualified spiritual person would cry out to God for the group and then things would be okay. The record indicates, though, that no one came forward, not even a leader. God kept waiting, but no one stepped up.

HE IS STILL LOOKING

Obviously, the times have changed, the locations are different, the nationalities are distinct, but the heart of the Father is the same. He is looking for someone to bridge the gap and stand before Him on behalf of the people. We can no longer hope someone else will step forward and intercede. We are responsible for this time; this is our watch, our moment. Things are not going to just work themselves out or simply get better. I have learned over the years that hope is good to have, but it is not a strategy.

We are in an epic battle with the enemy advancing and walking through the breaches in our walls. No longer can we look the other way, nor shrug off our personal responsibility.

I HAVE QUESTIONS

Where do you stand? You stand somewhere. We stand on ball-fields, service teams at church, work places, gyms, school meetings, community boards, and other places. However, are you consistently standing before God and crying out for His immediate intervention? Are you making intercession on behalf of the people you love, your church, your community, or your nation? If not, the enemy is poised to destroy everything in his path. He will show no mercy. He is ruthless and will not stop until everything is ruined.

Who will step up and stop the advancement of the aggressor? God wants to know? He asks, "Who will stand before me?" (v. 30)

God is not only waiting, but is looking for someone to come before Him. Will you be that person? If so, go ahead, take a moment and tell Him that you will be the one.

11

THIS IS WHAT CONCERNS ME THE MOST

"If man is man, and God is God, to live without prayer is not merely an awful thing; it is an infinitely foolish thing."
Phillips Brooks

The Medal of Honor is the most prestigious medal the President of the United States of America can bestow on one of its military personnel. It is reserved for those who in a time of war demonstrate extreme bravery, patriotism, valor, courage, and sacrifice.

Not everyone qualifies to receive this highly esteemed medal. It takes a special person. Below is one such individual that deserved the medal of honor award.

Staff Sgt. Ronald J. Shurer II served as a medical sergeant with Operational Detachment Alpha (ODA) 3336, Special Operations Task Force-11. On April 6, 2008, the ODA was on a mission to capture or kill high-value targets of the Hezeb Islami al Gulbadin in Shok Valley, Afghanistan.

As the ODA navigated through the valley, a series of insurgent sniper fire, rocket-propelled grenades, as well as small-arms and machine-gun fire forced the unit into a defensive fighting position. Around that time, Shurer received word that his forward-assault element was also pinned down at another location, and the forward team had sustained multiple casualties.

DECISIVE ACTION

With disregard for his safety, Shurer moved quickly through a hail of bullets toward the base of the mountain to reach the locked-down forward element. While on the move, Shurer stopped to treat a wounded teammate's neck injury caused by shrapnel from a recent rocket-propelled grenade blast. After providing aid, Shurer spent the next hour fighting across several hundred meters. Eventually, Shurer arrived to support the pinned-down element and immediately rendered aid to four critically wounded U.S. Soldiers and 10 injured Afghan commandos until teammates arrived. Soon after their arrival, the team sergeant was severely wounded, forcing Shurer to run 15 meters through a barrage of gunfire.

A TARGET FOR SNIPERS

As he exposed himself to the enemy, snipers took aim at Shurer, shooting him in the helmet and wounding his arm. Shurer made it to his teammate's location and pulled the sergeant to cover to render care.

Moments later, Shurer moved back through heavy gunfire to help sustain another teammate who suffered a traumatic wound to his right leg. For the next five and a half hours, Shurer helped keep the large insurgent force at bay while simultaneously providing care to his wounded teammates. Overall, Shurer's actions helped save the lives of all wounded casualties under his care.[21]

Currently, there are just over 3,500 soldiers who have received the medal of honor. It is truly given to those who are most honorable, having helped shape our nation's history, by either their acts of military valor, patriotism, bravery, and/or sacrifice.

------

[21] https://www.army.mil/medalofhonor/shurer/?from=features

LET'S BE HONEST

Prayer is a powerful weapon. We can touch heaven and influence God's work at every point on the earth. Our prayers not only commission angels, stop demonic advancements, neutralize evil, but they also empower missionaries, pastors, evangelists, and teachers. Our prayers move God! Additionally, our praying releases the irresistible conviction of the Holy Spirit upon sinners and prodigals alike. There is nothing like it on earth!

GOD WILL RECOGNIZE THOSE WHO HAVE MADE THE SACRIFICE SO OTHERS CAN LIVE

On that great and dreadful day when we stand before Jesus at the Bema Seat, God will reveal the most impactful contributors to the work of God on the earth. A brilliant methodical spectacle will unfold for all to see. Who will take center stage? Who will He recognize?

I am convinced it won't be the pastors, evangelists, teachers, prophets, or even apostles who will get the greatest recognition. It will be those who gave themselves to prayer. Yes, we are grateful for all the public gifts and the people who faithfully proclaimed the Word of God and who sacrificed greatly on many levels for the cause of Christ. Certainly, they will receive their recognition from the Lord. However, in my opinion, the true champions are those who never ascended the steps of a platform to address the awaiting audience, never glistened under the lights of a stage, or had their calendar filled with opportunities to travel abroad to testify and preach the good news. Most likely these individuals never received any attention or awards for their labor.

Throughout history, intercessors have been "behind the scenes" type of people - hidden. They were not well known to men, but they were and are well known by God. Here is what is so beautiful about these individuals: they have a history with God. They meet with Him regularly to contend for His cause. It is "these people" who in their prayer closet praying and wrestling against principalities, religious spirits, and demonic strongholds so God's message can be spoken and received with little to no resistance. The special group who answered the call to prayer will be the ones who will be asked to come to the front of the line, take the best seat, and perhaps sit closest to their Master. They are God's finest warriors!

Again, when we get to heaven and our time on earth is over, I think God will reveal to us the glorious impact the ministry of prayer has on the earth. He will point to it and say, "Because of your prayers look at what I was able to do!"

However, on the other side of this, I also think He will disclose to all of us the tragedy of limited prayer, half-hearted prayer, or even prayerlessness and its effect the earth. I think we will all be astonished as we stand before Him of all the things that could have been prevented on the earth and all the battles that could have been won if we had given ourselves to prayer.

Leonard Ravenhill stated, "Five minutes inside eternity and we will wish that we had sacrificed more, wept more, grieved more, loved and prayed more, and given more." It will not take long for us to realize we could have done more. Can you imagine the overwhelming sensation of regret when we see what could have been done for Him?

Dwight L. Moody once said, "Next to the wonder of seeing my Savior will be, I think, the wonder that I made so little use of the power of prayer."

12

IT'S A HOLY WAR

"I realize that many Christians have not been praying because they have not accepted the reality of war in which we find ourselves."
Francis Frangipane

"Reverend Lars Olsen Skrefsrud, Norwegian minister mightily used of God, was won to Christ through prevailing prayer warfare. An ordinary country girl, Bolette Hinderli, was praying once when she was given a vision of a prisoner in a prison cell. She could see his face and body in the vision. The voice seemed to say to her, "This man will share the same fate as other criminals if no one takes up the work of praying for him. Pray for him and I will send him out to proclaim my praises among the heathen." Bolette began to prevail in prayer. Day after day she held on for the salvation of this unknown prisoner. She waited and prayed and believed to hear some day of a convict who had become converted and called into missionary work. After a considerable time, she was visiting in Stavanger, Norway, when she heard that a converted former convict was to preach that evening in one of the churches. She went, and as soon as Skrefsrud stepped into the pulpit, she recognized him as the very person she had seen in her vision and for whom she had prevailed."[22]

What this little girl accomplished for the Kingdom of God is beyond noteworthy; it is, in fact, remarkable. This accomplishment for the Kingdom leads one to ask what would have happened had she not obeyed, followed-through, or simply disregarded what God had spoken to her. What if she had not prayed fervently for this man? The answer is in what she heard, *"This man will share the same fate as the other criminals if no one takes up the work of praying for him."* Praise God she listened and prayed! Her relentless work in prayer for this man not only spared his life, but God also saved him, and he began preaching the gospel!

This true story beautifully unveils to us the importance and necessity God places on prayer. Because she obeyed and prayed fervently, this man was not only saved, but he preached the gospel and thousands were added to the Kingdom of God.

---

[22] O. Hallesby, Prayer (London: Hodder & Stoughton, 1936), 103-104

I need you to grasp this truth...no matter how old or young you are, you can make a difference. You may not dawn a stage and speak in front of thousands of people, but you can influence and help those that do. As an intercessor, your work is more important than the one who minister in the public. Only heaven will reveal the full impact of a person who consistently and persistently prays. Their reward awaits them. The other high-profile figures that we all admire will have to step aside as the Lord parades in front of us all the true heroes of the faith - **Warrior Intercessors!** They are the secret agents that the Lord has used. They are the ones to cause the effectiveness of the gospel to go forth.

PRIMARY WEAPON GOD USES

I am afraid that too many believers do not understand two things: 1) We have significant role to play in the war with satan and his agenda. 2) The primary weapon God uses to neutralize the enemy is prayer.

Failing to fully comprehend the above places the church in a perpetual state of frustration. This frustration ultimately leaves us no other option other than continuing to prophesy about future moves of God while never stepping into one. Additionally, it causes the church to be on the defensive rather than the offensive. This is not only irresponsible, but dangerous on all levels.

The remarkable prayer champion Charles Spurgeon said, "He who knows how to overcome with God in prayer has heaven and earth at his disposal."[23] I don't know if the Bible could be more clear on this subject. Over and over the scriptures point us to His desire to answer our prayers. We must capitalize on this sweet invitation to partner with Him.

I feel Martin Luther said it best, "Prayer is not overcoming God's reluctance, but laying hold of His willingness." God is willing to do all He promised. He expectantly awaits our ask. He is on the ready to respond.

"We do not have because we do not ask."
James 4:2. (NIV)

Think about this - it is possible to pray with such effectiveness that satan has no option but to retreat and pull back his forces. He cannot remain nor prevail when there is a collection of believers who pray fervently and effectively.

Not only do our forceful prayers have the capacity to stagnate satan's advancements, but they also can actually force him to surrender

---

[23] Thomas Payne, *The Greatest Force on Earth*, 7th ed. (London: Marshall Brothers, n.d.), 20.

territory and retreat from his currently held positions. A. J. Gordon echoes, "We have authority to take from the enemy everything he is holding back. The chief way of taking is by prayer, and by whatever action prayer leads us to. The cry that should be ringing out today is the great cry, 'Take, in Jesus' great Name!'"[24]

THIS CHANGES EVERY THING

Look at this truth - when we pray the way James 5:16 instructs us to, with fervent prevailing prayers, we can actually drive satan out of the occupied territories of our families, friends, churches, and communities. Pushing back the enemy is absolutely possible. In fact, it is what God wants and needs us to do. He has given us the authority to remove and nullify the work of the devil. However, this is only accomplished when we fight on our knees.

We have to be resilient, patient and exercise strict discipline as we battle. It will be neither easy nor quick. It will take time to gain the victory! Here is why - in most cases the devil has had years to fortify his positions. He is entrenched.

However, everything shifts when we pray.

---

[24] Edwin and Lillian Harvey, Kneeling We Triumph (Chicago: Moody Press, 1974), 40.

HERE IS WHAT I KNOW

A. Satan never willingly gives up the territory he has gained. He has to be forced to surrender.

B. In many instances, satan has been granted legal access to certain people, places, and territories. This is a biblical concept. When the devil was tempting Jesus in Luke 4, the devil showed Jesus the kingdoms of the earth, and then he said, *"All this authority I will give You, and their glory; for this has been delivered to me, and I give it to whomever I wish."* (Luke 4:6)

The enemy possesses whatever a person surrenders to him. He walks through the doors we open and makes the place his own.

C. When a local church stands united in prayer and prays prevailing fervent prayers, satan will have no choice but to release his entrenched positions of influence. He will not be free to exercise his power at will. When we pray corporately, God sends forth His angels and releases His Holy Spirit to drive the enemy backwards.

D. If we fail to use the weapons available to us, then we cannot win the necessary battles in order to expand God's Kingdom. Therefore, the dark footprint of satan increases, and his territory expands.

J. C. Ryle amplified the same thought when he said, "Prayer has obtained things that seemed impossible and out of reach. It has won victories over fire, air, earth and water. Prayer opened the Red Sea. Prayer brought water from the rock and bread from Heaven. Prayer made the sun stand still. Prayer brought fire from the sky on Elijah's sacrifice. Prayer overthrew the army of Sennacherib. Prayer has healed the sick. Prayer has raised the dead. Prayer has procured the conversion of countless souls."[25]

My friend, prayer opens up heaven over our lives, family, and ministries. May the Lord prevail!

---

[25] J.C. Ryle. *A Call to Prayer*

13

SATAN RUNNING WITH HIS TAIL BETWEEN HIS LEGS

"God shapes the world by prayer. The more praying there is in the world the better the world will be, the mightier the forces against evil."
E.M. Bounds

Ray Steadman said, "Satan loves it when people think of prayer as a pitiful, pathetic, pointless gesture-and he hates it when people discover that prayer is direct access to the unlimited power of the one who formed the planets and hurled the stars through space." He adds, "What an exhilarating thought: When we pray, God listens! When we make our requests, God acts! Prayer is an essential link to God's active involvement in the world today."[26]

---

26 Ibid.

Let it be known that there is a type of praying that relentlessly assaults the kingdom of darkness. Not only does it disrupt the devil's agenda, but it also unleashes devastating results on his demonic schemes. What type of praying is this? It is called *Prevailing Fervent Prayer.*

I want you to get comfortable with this term and type of praying. It is a game changer on all fronts. Be warned that this type of praying doesn't come easy, but it is worth it.

Right now, as I write this, I feel the Lord's presence. I know God is summoning people all over the world who will be a part of the end-time army of intercessors. This rising group of intercessors are a select group of praying Lions! And this special remnant of Lions will boldly roar in the face of the devil as they intercede for the manifestation of the Kingdom of God upon the earth.

I know I have said this on multiple occasions, but I must drive this point home...*there is nothing the devil dreads more than a believer who prays fervently that God's will on the earth be done.* Make no mistake about it. Not only will our arch enemy do everything within his power to keep you from the place of intercession, but he will also keep you from this type of intercession. Why? Nothing torments him more than a saint who prays effectively; he and his kingdom bleed as result of it. They suffer and are tormented because of it.

REVENGE!

Has the devil abused you over the years? Has he stolen from you? Has he and his minions inflicted pained suffering on the ones you love? This kind of praying is the perfect opportunity to inflict pain and suffering back on him.

Think about this - it is possible to pray with such effectiveness that satan has no option but to retreat and pull back his forces. Not only do our forceful prayers have the capacity to stagnate satan's advancements, but they can actually force him to surrender territory and retreat from his currently held positions. He actually has to withdraw his troops because our efforts in prayer mobilizes heavenly resistance that stops his flow.

EVICTING THE SQUATTERS!

In our culture people can illegally live in homes that are vacant. They are what we call "squatters." They literally take up residence in an empty house, and the vagrants treat the home as if it is their home. In some states it is unlawful to evict such trespassers. I know this sounds crazy, but it is true. Usually, the court system has to get involved in order to force the squatters from the property. Then and only then are they required to move out. In other words, they have to be evicted by the authorities.

This is what fervent prevailing prayer does to the enemy.

KICKING DOWN WALLS

Here is some more great news! When we pray, we are not only halting the activity of the devil, but we are literally kicking down barriers and gates of fortified demonic strongholds. Every time we fervently pray and prevail in prayer, we weaken the satanic forces over us, our family, church and community. This is why consistency and longevity are necessary to any prayer group. We cannot be hit and miss in praying. Why? We are literally clearing the path for the thundering of God to resound over us and our area.

Knowing this, go ahead and prepare yourself for the fierce battle that will come. The devil will try to discourage you, frighten you, and even shame you. Your mind will be inundated with thoughts that divert your attention. You will be interrupted during prayer. You will face discouragement when you pray. You may even feel ineffective in prayer and believe that you are wasting your time. However, don't give into the temptation to give up. No! This is exactly what the devil wants! He wants you to quit praying. Successful kingdom intercessors anticipate the resistance; nevertheless, they press through it. They know that weariness, and confusion will also come, but they endure. My encouragement to you is embrace the struggle and don't relent - stay with it! It is in these times that you have to discipline yourself and intensify your resolve. Satan will do all he can to prevent you from getting to that place of "effective" praying.

THE MOST IMPORTANT THING WE DO

When the Saints of God are consistent in fervent praying, satan does not and cannot win. History records how God's power subdued entire cities because the people of that area prayed. However, if we fail to use the spiritual arsenal God left us, then we will not advance the Kingdom; therefore, we will not win.

Samuel Chadwick said, "It would seem as if the biggest thing in God's universe is a man who prays. There is only one thing more amazing, that is, that man, knowing this, should not pray."[27]

When missionary Jonathan Goforth wanted to begin a new work in North Honan Province in China, the infamous Hudson Taylor, who founded the Inland Mission, told him, "Brother, if you are to win that province you must go forward on your

---

[27] Samuel Chadwick, The Path of Prayer (Kansas City: Beacon Hill, 1931), 11–12.

knees."[28] Things haven't changed. Any true advancement of the Kingdom of God is always purchased and enforced on our knees.

Come on Lions ROAR!

[28] Gordan B. Watt, *Effectual Fervent Prayer*, (Woodland Park, CO.NGreat Commission) 84.

14

PINNING THE DEVIL

"Those who pray well, work well. Those who pray most, achieve the greatest results."
David McIntyre

Did you know the average person speaks around 16,000 words a day? Or, that the King James Bible contains 783,137 words? The novel *War and Peace* by Leo Tolstoy has 361 chapters, over 1,200 pages and contains 560,000 words. Are you impressed? As massive as that book is, it is not the largest book in the world. According to Guinness World Records, *In Search of Lost Time* by Marcel Proust is the world's longest book, with over 1.2 million words. If you read ten pages a day, it would take you over a year to read.

WORDS MATTER

According to David Trichet, "Words are the currency of communication. We use words to express what we think and how we feel."[29] Words describe and shape our thoughts, our perception, and even our understanding. I love the quote by Richard Rhodes, "Words are the model, words are the tools, words are the boards, words are the nails." How we choose and use words is important. Charles Capps adds, "Words are the most powerful thing in the universe...words are containers. They contain faith, or fear, and they produce after their kind."

Words paint pictures, tell a story, build suspense, and reveal intent. Even though they are just words, at times you can actually feel them; they carry weight and temperature. They guide and shape a person's perception while molding their ideals. Words can mend as well as tear down. Words affect us. It was Louisa May Alcott that said, "I like good strong words that mean something."

The Holy Spirit, who authored the Bible, chose His words carefully as men wrote them down. The Spirit selected words that mean something to describe what fervent prevailing prayer looks like. Here are just a few... **wrestling, agonizing, laboring, striving**. Also, terms like, **fight,**

[29] https://focus3.com/power-of-your-words/

warfare, struggle, stand, toil, weapons, always praying, take up your armor were used to describe a determined approach to prayer. These are more than words! These are stout and contentious words specifically given to us by the Holy Spirit. We must learn them and embrace their application to our lives.

What do these words have in common? Each one calls us to vigorous action; they place a demand on us to do something more than just passively lifting up our requests to God. These words sound a sobering alarm for believers to awaken to the seriousness of prayer.

AGONY

Did you know that fervent prevailing prayer is likened to agony or the activity of wrestling? In Luke 22:44, Jesus is in the Garden of Gethsemane prior to His arrest. It was here that the devil opposed Him. The Bible says as the full weight of the hours ahead pressed upon Jesus as He shed great drops of blood. It also says that Jesus *"being in an **agony,** he prayed more earnestly."*

Not only is this type of praying in the Bible, it is to emulated in our lives.

David Brainerd, who was a missionary to the Native Indians in the early 1700's, wrote that one time after praying, he found his heart "exceedingly enlarged in such anguish, and pleaded with so much sincerity and persistence" that when he got up from his knees, he felt extremely weak and overcome. He later said, "I could hardly walk straight. My joints were loose, sweat ran down my face and body, and my whole being seemed as if it would dissolve."[30]

Apostle Paul mentions that his associate Epaphras wrestled in prayer for the church at Colossae (Colossians 4:12 NIV), *"Epaphras, who is one of you and a servant of Christ Jesus, sends greetings. He is always **wrestling in prayer** for you, that you may stand firm in all the will of God, mature and fully assured."* The New King James Version puts it this way, *"Epaphras, who is one of you, a bondservant of Christ, greets you, **always laboring fervently for you in prayers...**"* These two translations not only highlight why he was praying but also the way Epaphras was praying. His prayer effort was likened to a wrestling match, a fight, and also to work/labor.

The Greek word used in both texts Luke 22 and Colossians 4 is *agonizomai.* You can actually see the word "agony" in the Greek word. The word, *agonizomai* is a direct reference to the very popular type of wrestling used during the Apostle Paul's era. It is interesting to note that each

---

[30] *Dr. Horton, Verbum Dei, p. 214.*

competitor would seek to neutralize his opponent by throwing him on the ground and putting a foot upon his neck. The competitor would seek full and total surrender from his opponent. This type of wrestling wasn't for the faint of heart and was widely popular. The contest would be tumultuous and combative; it will also require a great deal of exertion and effort in order to win. Again, the Holy Spirit chose this word to describe the type of praying He wants the Church to employ.

The Apostle Paul used this same word when he was encouraging Timothy, *"fight the good fight"* (1 Timothy 6:12), and once again when he told Timothy that he himself had "fought the good fight of faith (2 Timothy 4:2). The word choice by the Holy Spirit reveals to us the intense struggle we face in prayer.

HAND TO HAND COMBAT

When one embraces this level of prayer, it is like hand-to-hand combat with the enemy. You are standing toe-to-toe against the forces of evil, and you are literally pushing back on his agenda. And guess what? He doesn't like it; he pushes back!

Just as a wrestler wants to "pin" his opponent, we also want to "pin" or neutralize the work of the devil. However, this is hard work. For example, have you ever witnessed a wrestling match in person. The amount of energy exerted in the contest is epic. Feverishly, each combatant is trying to gain the advantage over the other. Each participant in a massive struggle to win. After each round, they are winded, gasping for breath. They gasp for air not because they are out of shape, or unfit for the moment. No! They are exhausted because they are trying to "pin" their opponent with all of their might.

Prayer is a bare-knuckle fight with the winner taking all the spoils. Prayer is an all-out war. Prayer isn't for the faint hearted or the self-seeking casual Christian. Martin Luther understood the full weight that is carried by an intercessor, "Prayer is indeed a continuous violent action of the spirit as it is lifted up to God. This action is comparable to that of a ship going against the stream."[31] Don't miss what Luther said, "It is a continuous violent action." Again, prayer is a "Close-quarters combat!" Think about it! While you and I are praying for God's will to be done on the earth, we are literally wrestling with opposing forces that seek the exact opposite. They (demons) want their will to be done, and they are committed to making sure it is.

IT IS WORTH IT

---

[31] Donald G. Bloesch, *Struggle of Prayer* (Colorado Springs: Helmers and Howard, 1988), 132.

You have to believe this. The commitment required of us and the sacrifice that is necessary will be worth it. When we submit to the level of prayer required, we will dislodge satan's fierce grip over people, regions, churches, and communities. It can even loosen satan's vice over political structures. Think about the possibilities!

Eric Ludy said, "Prayer is not some bb gun that God has given us to try to shoo away raccoons in the night. Prayer is nuclear power, world renovating in its epic strength. When used according to the pattern of Scripture, prayer alters history, alters the natural world, and alters the human soul." He adds, "The Sword of the Spirit is too heavy for a mere man to carry, but prayer enables us to lift it, swing it, and transform the world around us with it. Prayer is the catalyst behind everything Godly taking place in the earth."[32]

Wrestling prayer accomplishes much. It is one of the highest and effective forms of prayer. This is a confrontational type of prayer. As mentioned above, at times prayer can be fierce, ugly, vocal, painful, and exhausting as one boldly asserts the King's demands into and over situations.

------

[32] https://goodnessofgodministries.international/2011/09/25/lionhearted-prayer-warriors-for-God-the-legendary-heroes-of-all-generations/

I LOVE IT!

Wesley L. Duewel said, "The most important measure of prayer is not its length but its depth; not its beautiful words but its intensity. It is not necessarily a matter of how many hours you pray, but how intensely you pray when you do pray. There is a dynamic of perseverance—prayer must often be continued at some length, but whether short or long, let your prayer be fervent."[33]

I, as well as our people, have been engaged in this type of prayer on many occasions, especially at the North Georgia Revival. Afterwards I feel depleted physically; my mind is exhausted, but in my spirit, I knew a great victory had been won. Often, you don't know what that victory will look like beforehand, but when it happens you can trace it back to that specific time of intercession.

THIS IS OUR ONLY OPTION

We have no option but to take up the mighty mantle of fervent prevailing prayer. We must joyfully enlist into this army and enter the battlefield. Around the world the cause of Christ faces many roadblocks, setbacks, as the opposing forces have mounted a successful and

---

[33] Duewel, Wesley L.. Mighty Prevailing Prayer: Experiencing the Power of Answered Prayer (p. 76). HarperCollins Christian Publishing. Kindle Edition.

aggressive offensive campaign to blanket the world in wickedness. The devil has also coordinated an elaborate defensive posture on multiple fronts which has and continues to prohibit the advancement of the cause of Christ. Again, we must prevail in prayer for situations where God's will has been thwarted, and where satan has delayed and blocked Christ's cause.

We all know too well that there is both a spiritual and natural opposition to genuine moves of the Holy Spirit. When we faithfully pray, we mow down the obstacles that stand in the way of the gospel and revival.

15

BACK UP, PACK UP AND CLEAR OUT!

"There is no way to learn to pray but by praying."
Samuel Chadwick

Recently, after a horrific mass shooting that took numerous lives, a television news anchor negatively, but rightly, responded to the people who repeatedly called for prayer. She said, "Why do they [Christians] always pray after the tragedy, it's too late?"

I think she is partly right.

Yes, we do need to pray for those who were affected by the shooting, but she makes a valid point. What if we had prayed beforehand?

Perhaps the event could have been prevented altogether.

Truthfully, prayer is too often used reactively rather than proactively. Isn't it true we are quick to pray after a tragedy or when an unexpected crisis hits our lives? This is called defensive praying. This is fine and needed; however, the church must go on the offensive. This means taking the fight to the devil, hitting him with an aggressive prayer effort so the cause of Christ can advance and the enemies plans get averted. This is not just an idea; it is absolutely possible.

The early church utilized both defensive and offensive prayer positions. For example, when Peter and John were released by the authorities after being interrogated for causing a civil disruption as a result of a miracle that occurred at the gate Beautiful in Acts 3, the whole church gathered to pray. They prayed an aggressive offensive prayer. (Acts 4:23-24; 30-31)

> *23. And being let go, they went to their own companions and reported all that the chief priests and elders had said to them. 24 So when they heard that, they raised their voice to God with one accord and said: "Lord, You are God, who made heaven and earth and the sea, and all that is in them... 29 Now, Lord, look on their threats, and **grant to Your servants that with all boldness***

they may speak Your word, 30 by stretching out Your hand to heal, and that signs and wonders may be done through the name of Your holy Servant Jesus."

31 And when they had prayed, the place where they were assembled together was shaken; and they were all filled with the Holy Spirit, and they spoke the word of God with boldness."

Those that gathered to pray didn't settle, and certainly they were not measured in their requests. No, they prayed bold, courageous, and adventurous prayers. In other words, "God, let's do something consequential, monumental, and explosive. God massively use us!"

THE RISE OF THE RESISTANCE

The Bible makes it clear that our posture as believers is to resist and stand in opposition to all that satan imposes. We must take this seriously. However, doesn't it seem that satan's agenda is going virtually unopposed?

James 4:7 sheds light on this, *"Therefore submit to God. Resist the devil and he will flee from you."* The New English Bible translates verse 7 this way, **"Stand up to the devil and he will** *turn and run."* This is an explosive truth. I love it! If we resist him, he will TURN AND RUN! I think it is time that our actions cause the devil to turn and run. Something is stirring in the body of Christ. I feel it! A growing number of believers are joining the resistance movement - a prayer movement that resists satan's plans and releases the will of God. The Resistance is Rising!

WARNING: There is no doubt the devil commissions his highest generals and most seasoned demons to attack the spirit of prayer. Why? If he is successful at preventing churches from launching prayer meetings, then he has nothing to worry about; he wins.

Let this percolate in your mind. When we don't pray fervent prevailing prayers and don't resist his maneuvers and plans, we actually become submissive to the devil's will. Our prayer inactivity actually sends the signal that we are fine with what he is doing. And to take this thought even further, our lack of prayer engagement makes us somewhat complicit with what he is doing. How is this possible? Silence is deemed quiet support. Have you ever thought about it that way? We basically say, "All is well. Carry on. All is good."

GOOD NEWS: When we pray effectively, our prayers raise a wall against satan's strategies, desires, and schemes. His wishes for destruction fall short; he literally has to go back to the drawing board to work up a new plan. Again, I need you to grab this truth: the will of the devil gets frustrated when we pray effectively. It is as if the Lord, through our prayers, is raising up an opposing standard against the enemy (Isaiah 59:19). Fervent prevailing prayer puts a "check-mate" on the devil and loudly proclaims, "THUS FAR AND NO MORE!

Arthur Mathews wrote years ago, "In any situation where Satan dominates and threatens, God looks for a man through whom He may declare war on the enemy. He purposes that through that man Satan be served notice to back up, pack up, and clear out."[34]

It is time to aggressively do what Arthur Mathews suggested. It is time to serve the devil notice: **"BACK UP, PACK UP, and CLEAR OUT!"** Go ahead tell him right now, "devil, *back up, pack up, and clear out."* Say it as often as you need to. Say it until he obeys your command! Declare it over your family, church, and community.

Now is the perfect season to assume the posture of a warrior. Let's rise up and demand the Lord's will be done on the earth. I believe we all would

---

[34] Thomas Payne, *Greatest Force on Earth*, (Morgan and Scott, Ltd)122.

agree that this is not only the most important time in history. It also is the most important time of our lives. Let's stop living by fate and watching from the sidelines. May we begin to live by an aggressive faith that executes the plans of God on the earth.

The famed R. A. Torrey understood the power of aggressive fervent praying when he wrote, "The prayer that prevails with God is the prayer into which we put our whole soul, stretching out toward God in intense and agonizing desire.... If we put so little heart into our prayers, we cannot expect God to put much heart into answering them.... When we learn to come to God with an intensity of desire that wrings the soul, then shall we know a power in prayer that most of us do not know now."[35]

---

[35] R. A. Torrey, How to Pray (Chicago: Moody, 1900), 33–34.

16

THE POWER OF
THE GROUP

"Prayer is the mightiest power on earth. Enough of us, if we prayed enough, could save the world—if we prayed enough!"
Frank Laubach

There is something to be said about the force of a group when they gather around a common cause. The group, if lead correctly, can bring about significant change. The anthropologist Margaret Mead rightfully said, "Never doubt that a small group of thoughtful, committed citizens can change the world; indeed, it's the only thing that ever has."

THE GROUP

It is quite alarming how many churches do not have a weekly scheduled corporate (group) prayer meeting. Often, the leadership finds it difficult to schedule another meeting in an already packed church ministry schedule. Since, prayer meetings are usually the least attended church activity, more times than not, the prayer meeting becomes the least prioritized ministry. Therefore, the leaders leave it up to each person to govern their prayer life and hopefully that includes praying for the church.

I was troubled recently when a friend of mine shared this text thread he had with one of the senior pastors where he attended. Mind you, this church has multiple campuses and thousands of people attend their weekend worship services. My friend, who was learning the power of corporate prayer, was inquiring to see if his church could start a corporate prayer meeting:

Friend: Hey, my wife and I are interested in leading a prayer group at the church.

Sr. Minister: Also...talked to the Lead Pastor again about the daily prayer time. He is absolutely fine with anyone coming to the church and praying. I have talked with him about you and (your wife) and your passion for prayer as the catalyst of everything we do. Love that about you both and your passion for it, as it is critical for our spiritual growth. *He (Lead Pastor) did state there would likely never be a dedicated prayer program established at (name of church)*, but the open invitation would always be there for anyone to come and pray when they wanted.

The beginning of the pastor's response was cordial and complimentary; however, the last portion of his text sadly made my heart shutter. The pastor said, "…there would likely never be a **dedicated prayer program** established at…"

How does the pastor's response make you feel?

Let me be clear when I say that this is how too many churches actually feel about prayer. Pastors know prayer has a place in a person's personal life, but it is not important enough or it's too complicated for them to corporately gather for it. This breaks the Father's heart. Jesus and the early church modeled something entirely different than what we are seeing demonstrated in many churches. They prayed together.

This is how Leonard Ravenhill looked at ministries and churches who don't prioritize corporate prayer.

Take a look:

"The Cinderella of the Church today is the prayer meeting. This handmaid of the Lord is unloved and unwooed because she is not dripping with pearls of intellectualism, nor glamorous with the silks of philosophy, neither is she enchanting with the tiara of psychology. She wears the homespuns of sincerity and humility and so is not afraid to kneel!

He continues his thoughts:

"Poverty-stricken as the Church is today in many things, she is most stricken here, in the place of prayer. We have many organizers, but few agonizers; many players and payers, few prayers; many singers, few clingers; lots of pastors, few wrestlers; many fears, few tears; much fashion, little passion; many interferers, few intercessors; many writers, but few fighters. Failing here, we fail everywhere."

He adds:
"The ministry of preaching is open to few; the ministry of prayer - the highest ministry of all human offices is open to all. Spiritual adolescents say, 'I'll not go tonight, it's only the prayer meeting.' It may be that satan has little cause to fear most preaching. Yet past experiences sting him to rally all his infernal army to fight against God's people praying."[36]

---

[36] Leonaard Ravenhill, (excerpted from I (Bethany House Publishers)

Jim Cymbala made an acute observation regarding the modern local church. He states, "What does it say about our churches today that God birthed the church in a prayer meeting, and prayer meetings today are almost extinct?"[37]

This is a terrible indictment against the church; however, sadly, it is true.

I wonder how much of the work of God has gone unrealized and unfulfilled because leaders have minimized, or worse yet, not implemented a corporate prayer meeting? This can neither be our position nor our practice any longer. Prayerless churches are unacceptable in this hour.

NEUTRALIZING DEMONS

I liken corporate prayer meetings to the strategic ministry of John the Baptist. As we all know, John the Baptist was given the assignment to prepare the way of the Lord Jesus. He came before the Lord to "make straight" the way, or in other words, "clear the way" for the Messiah. In essence, John the Baptist's ministry prepared the hearts of the people to receive the Messiah. Prayer does the same thing. When correctly appropriated, prayer clears the way for the

---

[37] Kevin W. Shorter, *Prayer Quotes: inspiration to Draw You Closer to God* . Kindle Edition.

Kingdom to advance forcefully with little to no resistance.

We acknowledge in every region there are demonic strongholds and resistances to the work of God. This resistance can be multiple controlling spirits in the atmosphere and/or an embedded religious spirit in the local church. It is a proven fact that when a church prays together, it is an empowered assault on all demonic entities and strongholds in the area. Every single time we gather for prayer the enemy is aware of it. He feels it, and, to some degree, suffers from it.

THIS IS WHAT COULD HAPPEN

In his book, Wesley Duewel tells a story of the power of prevailing prayer in a corporate prayer meeting:

> An Anglican church in Britain many years ago had a prayer meeting each Sunday morning before the eight o'clock Communion service. As the people arose from their knees one Sunday, a man asked the pastor, "I wish you would pray for my boy. He is twenty-two years old now and has not been to church for years." The pastor proposed that they stop immediately and pray for five minutes.

They earnestly united together in prayer. Nothing was said to the young man, but that night he came to the church, was deeply convicted by the message, stayed behind brokenhearted, and received Christ as his Savior. The next morning one of the church staff said to the pastor, "That conversion last night is a challenge to prayer—a challenge from God. Shall we accept it?" "What do you mean?" asked the pastor. "Well," he said, "shall we single out the worst man in the parish and pray for him?" After discussion, they all decided on a Mr. K. as the most sinful person they knew. They all agreed together in prayer for his conversion and began to hold on in prayer each day. At the end of the week, during a Saturday night prayer meeting, while someone was actually praying by name for this man, the door swung open, and in he staggered in a very intoxicated condition. He had never been inside the building before. Without removing his cap, he sat on a chair and buried his face in his hands. Before the prayer meeting was over, God had sobered the man and saved him, and he later became a Christian worker.[38]

---

[38] Duewel, Wesley L.. Mighty Prevailing Prayer: Experiencing the Power of Answered Prayer (pp. 147-148). HarperCollins Christian Publishing. Kindle Edition.

May every church have a corporate prayer meeting, and may we become so bold and effective in our prayer meetings that we begin to have a top ten list of biggest targets we want to get saved or have an encounter with God.

If we will do our part, God will do His!

17

BEHIND THE CURTAIN

"Prayer is not overcoming God's reluctance, but laying hold of His willingness."
Martin Luther

I begin this chapter with two quotes that have the potential to reshape the contemporary mindset regarding corporate prayer meetings.

A. The revival historian J. Edwin Orr stated, "No great spiritual awakening has begun anywhere in the world apart from united prayer—Christians persistently praying for revival."[39]

---

[39] J. Oswald Sanders, *Prayer Power Unlimited*, (Grand Rapids: Discovery House Publishers), 120.

B. Andrew Murray said, "The man who mobilizes the Christian church to pray will make the greatest contribution to world evangelization in history."

These statements need to be unpacked and are worthy of further meditation. In addition, fully understanding them will have profound implications on the body of Christ.

Charles Spurgeon who was one of the finest preachers of all time and who experienced sustained revival led a prayer meeting every Monday night in which over 1,000 people attended.[40] Below is one of his most profound statements regarding prayer.

> "As a church, we have been specially favored; but we have not exhausted the possibilities of prosperity, or the resources of heavenly power. There is a future for us, if we pray. Greater things than these lie behind that curtain; no hand can unveil them but the hand of prayer. The singular blessings which have rested upon us in the past call upon us to pray; the marked prosperity and unity of the present invite us to pray; and the hopes of the future encourage us to pray. Behold, the Lord says to you, "Ask, and ye shall receive." Brothers, sisters, slack not your asking;

[40] David Bryant, *Kneeling Christian*, 11.

but, for the love of souls, multiply your petitions, and increase your importunity."[41]

Did you catch it? I want to highlight what Spurgeon said again,

"Greater things than *these lie behind that curtain;* no hand can unveil them but the hand of prayer."

Spurgeon is sharing with us a profound revelation about one of the purposes of prayer. There are things that need to come out from BEHIND THE CURTAIN and only the "hand of prayer" reveals and releases the "greater things" behind the curtain. Satan knows this and wants to keep the things of power behind the curtain, so he unleashes all of his resources to keep us from the place of prayer.

Yes, God answers prayers of the individual, but there is something extra special when people gather around the altar for a season of prayer. The truth of Ecclesiastes 4:12 becomes apparent, *"Though one may be overpowered by another, two can withstand him. And a threefold cord is not quickly broken."*

---

[41] Spurgeon, C. H.. Only a Prayer-Meeting! (p. 164). CrossReach Publications. Kindle Edition.

NUMBERS DO MATTER

Whenever there is a war, numbers matter. You want to overpower the enemy and render him powerless or scurrying for cover. Deuteronomy 32:30 states that *"one shall put 1,000 to flight, but two shall put 10,000 to flight."* This text validates the significance of more than just one person standing in the place of prayer. When two people come together to pray, it doesn't double the power and influence. It multiplies it ten-fold. The devil knows this and fears groups that pray prevailing prayers. He discourages it at every turn.

The following words from R.A. Torrey capture this sentiment, "When the devil sees a man or woman who really believes in prayer, who knows how to pray, and who really does pray, and, above all, when he sees a whole church on its face before God in prayer, he trembles as much as he ever did, for he knows that his day in that church or community is at an end."[42]

Andrew Bonar said, "The Prince of the power of the air seems to bend all the force of his attack against the spirit of prayer."[43]

---

[42] Ibid.

[43] Kevin W. Shorter, *Prayer Quotes: inspiration to Draw You Closer to God* . Kindle Edition.

J. Oswald Sanders stated, "There is a cumulative effect in prayer. The focusing of many prayers on one life or on a situation can change defeat into victory."[44] Don't miss what he said. When a group focuses on a specific issue or person in prayer that person or circumstance will change. The power of the masses matter, and it gets things done that otherwise are too difficult or too large for one person.

You see, our goal isn't to simply gather together for another meeting, there is a greater purpose. We want to pray with such effectiveness that we overwhelm the dark realm with a supernatural display of force and power. We long for our prayer meetings to be destructive to all things satan has done and is doing.

---

[44] J. Oswald Sanders, *Prayer Power Unlimited*, (Grand Rapids: Discovery House Publishers), 139.

18

PRAYER FACTORIES

"We have taught people how to witness, teach, serve, and even play an instrument, but have we taught our people to pray?"
Todd Smith

A.W. Tozer said, "The Christian is a holy rebel loose in the world with access to the throne of God."

Oh wow, did you catch that? You may want to read it again. Have you ever looked at who you are in that light? It is true. You are a HOLY REBEL! A praying HOLY REBEL. I love it! Tozer continues his thought, "Since prayer is detrimental to the evil one's purposes, satan and his minions do their utmost to interfere when we pray especially opposing us when we try to take time for prayer because the enemy knows better than most Christian's the power of persistent prayer!"[45]

Lean in as you read the next section:

The whole world will benefit when we pray. There is NOTHING that has a greater impact upon our current world and the advancement of Kingdom of God like intercession. The good news is that God is no respecter of persons, and He will respond to any believer that commits himself/herself to prayer.

But, be warned! Satan loathes prayer, and he will do all in his power to keep you from it. Andrew Murray said, "Satan will bring forth all his power to prevent us from becoming men of prayer."[46] The enemy knows that prayer is the secret to stopping his vile intentions.

Prevailing prayer to satan is the most feared of all ministries within the church. Why? Fervent prayer is a heavenly fiery engagement toward the agenda and forces of hell. This kind of prayer stands in the way of his goals for you and your family. When we give ourselves to prayer and

---

[45] https://goodnessofgodministries.international/2011/09/25/lionhearted-prayer-warriors-for-God-the-legendary-heroes-of-all-generations/

[46] Andrew Murray, Prayer Life, (Chicago: Moody)1 27.

---

pray with authority and faith, the devil doesn't know what to do with it. It throws his plans in disarray.

Prayer was not only the foundation of the Church's existence over 2,000 years ago, but the catalyst of her triumph, glistening like gold. All of the brightest and most effective moves of God the world has ever known can be traced back to prayer. It is the heartbeat of every heaven-sent revival.

I am going to say it - churches need to become "PRAYER FACTORIES." What do I mean? The primary function of a factory is to transform raw materials into finished products.

We cannot miss this window of opportunity to produce praying saints. The mandate on the local church is to teach the people under their care to pray. We must we teach people how to pray effectively because effective praying does not come naturally to us. It must be learned.

This includes all age groups even the little ones.

THE SHOES AT THE DOOR

When I make my way to join my church family for prayer each Sunday morning, I pass by our children's sanctuary. As I make my way down the hallway, I see shoes stacked up outside their sanctuary door. Our children have come an hour early to pray. Before they enter their sanctuary to pray, they take their shoes off. Often, I stick my head inside the door, and I see the children on their faces crying out for a move of God to take place in their service.

One of the most difficult tasks a leader will undertake is to teach people to pray. Not only will it take time and a lot of energy, but there will also be extreme highs and deep lows, exciting days as well as disappointing times. Jesus knew these emotions all too well. Remember when He asked His disciples to pray with Him in the Garden of Gethsemane? He was at a pivotal moment His life and needed His closest friends to pray. The disciples started strong but quickly fell asleep. Jesus rebuked them for their inability to tarry with Him for one hour.

WHOSE FAULT IS IT?

Tragically, most adults don't know how to pray effectively because it was not modeled or taught consistently from their church leaders. This has to change immediately. Why? PRAYER IS OUR MOST IMPORTANT WORK! Lou Engle said, "We have taught a generation to feast and play but the times demand we fast and pray."

We have to teach people how to pray. We cannot leave the blessed followers of Christ who are under our care to figure out this essential necessity on their own. It is too important and too much is at stake.

NOTE: The Lead Pastor has to become the primary prayer minister. I know from first-hand experience the local church prayer ministry will never reach its full potential without the Lead Pastor becoming the Lead Intercessor. Pastors must be engaged and do more than announce the time and location of the prayer meeting. We have to attend and pray fervently.

Prayer can no longer be secondary, something we do when all else is done. It can no longer fall behind study, sermon preparation, and ministry obligations. It must be primary. Prayer has to be elevated and celebrated.

THE WORLD IS ON FIRE

If I may so bold to say, having a minimal prayer effort personally and corporately is like using a squirt gun to try to put out an apartment fire. It helps but won't put out the fire.

The world is on fire. Everywhere darkness is bellowing and swallowing up our communities and families. In all honestly, it is a wildfire and out of control, and in an unprecedented ferociousness, darkness is destroying everything in its path. The devil's tactics are schemed and precise. Methodically, he is influencing every segment of our society. Never in the history of the world has there been so much evil on the earth. Things are not just bad; they are really bad. However, I am not discouraged at all. Here is why? I have seen first-hand what prayer can do. The North Georgia Revival has witnessed the result of praying people. God has changed the lives of tens of thousands of people because our people pray.

The only remedy to the world situation is the praying church. Nothing else will stop satan's plans - not our preaching, not our worship, not our programs, not our outreaches, not our good intentions. Nothing but prayer will stop him. Please hear my heart when I say that all the aforementioned ministries are vital and must continue; however, the prayer ministry of the local church is the platform that the other necessary ministries stand upon. Prayer is the fuel to the fire.

Andrew Murray once said, "Where ... we work more than we pray, the presence and the power of God are not seen in our work as we would wish."[47] I have experienced far too often the effects of a deficit of prayer. I have felt the absence of the presence of God on my ministry and preaching. There is a void. It is a terrible

---

[47] Andrew Murray, *Ministry of Intercession* (New York: Revell, 1898), 13-14

feeling. And what is most terrible is that the people I deeply love were affected by the deficit.

If Church history has taught us anything it is this: the release of God's power upon the earth is directly connected to prayer. Edward Payson rightfully said, "If we would do much for God, we must ask much of God: we must be men of prayer."

19

JAMES DIDN'T HAVE TO DIE!

"The man who mobilizes the Christian church to pray will make the greatest contribution to the world evangelization in history."
Andrew Murray

One of the most alarming events of the New Testament is when James is put to death by Herod in Acts 12. Herod didn't kill just anybody; he killed James. James was in Jesus' inner circle and one of His closest friends. This is tragic because James was murdered just a few years into his ministry.

What happened?

Why did this occur?

How could this even happen?

I will answer those questions shortly, but let's continue the story.

When King Herod saw how James' death pleased the people, he forthrightly arrested Peter. His goal? To make Peter the next martyr of the newly founded movement. His undeniable intention was to kill Peter - the Rock, another one in Jesus' band of brothers.

However, something was different this time. The church wasn't a by-stander waiting on God to save one of His choice servants. No! This time they prayed; they prevailed in prayer. Notice, verse 5 of Acts 12 states that *"**constant** prayer was made for Peter by the church."* This is a huge revelation on the value God places on prayer.

In referring to the type of prayer, the Greek word for "constant" is *ek-ten-ace'* and it means **"stretched out, intentional, earnest, fervent, much prayer**." At first, you notice what this prayer is not. It isn't casual, disengaged, mundane, or soft; it is simply not mere words. No! It was assiduous and attentive. It was a relentless bombardment of the throne of God by a group of people on behalf of their beloved friend, demanding his release. The church in Acts 12 was awakened to the severity of the moment and refused to allow Peter to be a victim of Herod's thirst for blood. They chose spiritual aggression over spiritual laziness. They took the offensive and displayed the power of "prevailing prayer." When the church prayed heaven responded.

God sent an angel to wake Peter from a deep sleep. The angel told Peter that it was time to go. The two of them walked completely undetected out of the prison, through the dark streets of the city, and eventually they ended up at the very house where the church had been praying for them. What a scene! God answered the prayers of His church.

What an incredible moment! What an awesome expression of faith! The church prevailed!

Here is sobering note: There is no mention that the church prayed for James the Apostle. Perhaps a few did, but there is no biblical text that indicates that the church gathered to pray for him. The result? He died. James was executed! I have the conviction that James died prematurely because the church did not pray for him. Is that even possible? I believe it is.

BRACE YOURSELF

You won't hear this in many places, but the following statements are true and are validated through various Biblical texts and real-world experiences.

When we neglect prayer, either intentionally or unintentionally, devastating consequences can and will occur. This truth, regretfully, is demonstrated before our eyes every day. Additionally, when we pray half-heartedly, calamitous and ruinous events can take place that alter lives and abort God's plans. Frankly, if we are honest, much of the disastrous events that happen in our nation and communities can be traced back to a lack of prayer by the Church. This must change!

PAY CLOSE ATTENTION TO THE TUG

The Lord may tug on your heart to suddenly pray for someone or something. This can happen to us at any moment while driving down the road, while at work, while at the ball field, and even while we are asleep. Many of us have been awakened suddenly from our deep sleep to only wonder why. There is a purpose for this; somebody needs you to pray. There is no such thing as "coincidences." God is needing you to stop what you are doing and pray. We have to take this seriously.

John Wesley said, "God responds to prayers of His people." Again, when we suddenly feel the Holy Spirit nudging us to pray, it is an indication something is about to happen or something is already taking place. When we obey this call to prayer, we are engaging in real-time spiritual warfare. There is a battle in the heavenly realm, and our prayers influence the battle.

We must become more familiar and sensitive to the nudging of the Holy Spirit in this area. When we obey these promptings and give ourselves to prayer, God's purposes can be executed and the devil's plan averted. We must realize this truth spoken by Duewel Wesley, "It [prayer] is God's chosen way to bring heaven's power, heaven's resources, and heaven's angels into action on earth."[48]

Our immediate intercession can dispatch angels, resources, and God's power whenever there is a need or crisis. For example, a missionary on furlough told the following true story while visiting his home church in Michigan:

> "While serving at a small field hospital in Africa, every two weeks I traveled by bicycle through the jungle to a nearby city for supplies. This was a journey of two days and required camping overnight at the halfway point. On one of these journeys, I arrived in the city where I planned to collect money from a bank, purchase medicine, and supplies, and then

---

[48] Duewel, Wesley L.. Mighty Prevailing Prayer: Experiencing the Power of Answered Prayer (p. 19). HarperCollins Christian Publishing. Kindle Edition.

begin my two-day journey back to the field hospital.

"Upon arrival in the city, I observed two men fighting, one of whom had been seriously injured. I treated him for his injuries and at the same time talked to him about the Lord. I then traveled two days, camping overnight, and arrived home without incident...

"Two weeks later I repeated my journey. Upon arriving in the city, I was approached by the young man I had treated. He told me that he had known I carried money and medicines. He said, 'Some friends and I followed you into the jungle, knowing you would camp overnight. We planned to kill you and take your money and the drugs. But just as we were about to move into your camp, we saw that 26 armed guards surrounded you.' At this I laughed and said that I was certainly all alone in that jungle campsite.

"The young man pressed the point, however, and said, 'No, sir, I was not the only person to see the guards; my friends also saw them and we all counted them. It was because of those guards that we were afraid and left you alone.'

"At this point in the sermon, one of the men in the congregation jumped to his feet and interrupted the missionary and asked if he could tell him the exact day this happened? The missionary told the congregation the date and the man who interrupted told him this story.

"On the night of your incident in Africa it was morning here and I was playing golf. I was about to putt when I felt the urge to pray for you. In fact, the urging of the Lord was so strong I called some men in this church to meet with me at the church to pray for you. Would all of those men who met with me on that day stand up?"

The men who met together to pray all stood up. The missionary wasn't concerned with who they were; he was too busy counting how many men he saw. There were 26 men who stood!

This story is remarkable. It goes without saying, but we have to develop a greater sensitivity to the prompting of the Holy Spirit. We have to obey the urge. Consequently, to ignore it could be tragic for yourself, the ones you love, a missionary, or a community. Moreover, to push it aside and not obey could mean a someone may suffer unnecessarily or die prematurely.

Your prayers may avert a tragedy.

OBEY THE URGE!

20

I WANT SOME ICE CREAM!

"When a Christian shuns fellowship with other Christians, the devil smiles. When he stops studying the Bible, the devil laughs. When he stops praying, the devil shouts for joy."
Corrie ten Boom

In the United States, we eat our fair share of ice cream. According to the International Dairy Foods Association, the average American consumes 20 pounds of ice cream (four gallons) in a year.[49] I have great news for you. You no longer have to feel bad when you eat ice cream! Researchers have found that ice cream has several health benefits such as probiotics which improves gut health, and calcium that strengthens bones and teeth. Ice cream also

---

[49] https://www.canr.msu.edu/news/the-surprising-health-benefits-of-eating-ice-cream

contains vitamins A, D, and B12 which boosts your immune system.[50]

I can assume from my limited and selective research that eating ice cream makes one healthier and less likely to become sick. This fact, my friend, was worth your investment in this book!

Eating ice cream is such a wonderful experience. In 1984, July was designated National Ice Cream Month, and each year, the third Sunday of the month is National Ice Cream Day!

What is your favorite flavor? Mine is chocolate while Karen's is vanilla. I still get excited about a double scoop of chocolate ice cream on a waffle cone. It is one of God's greatest gifts to mankind. Isn't it true that while you are eating ice cream that all the cares of the world seem to disappear!

Nobody loves ice cream more than children. And we as parents know that children understand the principle of persistence. For example, when a child asks a parent or grandparent for ice cream and the answer is "no," what usually happens? In short order, the child asks again. The parent gives another resounding "no." What happens next? The child asks yet again. The child doesn't take "no" or "delay" as the final outcome. Eventually, in many cases, guess what happens?

---

[50] Ibid.

The child is sitting and enjoying a scoop of ice cream.

It's undeniable that at no point in the child's request of ice cream do they not believe it is going to happen. The repetitive requests aren't a sign of a lack of faith, but actually the opposite. They keep asking because they know eventually their parent will give them ice cream.

ASK AGAIN, IT IS A SIGN OF FAITH

Somewhere along the way, we were taught it was an indication that you had imbedded doubt in your heart if you asked God for something more than once. In other words, you were not demonstrating faith, but faithlessness. Scripturally, this is incorrect.

When a child incessantly asks for something, it is an expression of their faith. They fully believe if they keep asking, they will receive.

Prevailing persistent prayer chooses to keep asking and will not relent no matter what is seen with our eyes or how we feel.

DELAY? IT JUST MAY BE SATAN

There are many reasons why we must be persistent when we pray. Here is one: When we pray, in real time, we frustrate satan's strategies. As a reminder, satan actually can interfere with our prayers and delay the response from heaven.

Recall what happened when Daniel prayed (Daniel 10), the angel said, "*Since the first day that you set your mind ... to humble yourself before your God, your words were heard, and I have come in response to them*" (Dan. 10:12). But the angel revealed that a demonic ruler "*resisted me twenty-one days*" until Michael, another archangel, came to help him (v. 13). The answer came three weeks later, twenty-one intense days of delay.

We must remember that when we pray, we effect three kingdoms: the heavenly, the demonic, and the earthly. The earthly and demonic kingdom will naturally resist your prayers. There are opposing forces that refuse to yield territory. These three worlds are in constant conflict with each other; therefore, we have to keep praying, remain diligent, be steadfast while we execute the will of God in prayer. Patience is a virtue and a necessary component if you are serious about prayer. We need it in order to not give up.

How long will it take to get an answer? I can't answer that question precisely. Each situation has various extenuating circumstances. This is a great mystery and resilient faith is necessary to endure between the ask and the receiving. We cannot afford for our hearts to faint in the space between the two realities. This is why Jesus said, *"Men should always pray and not give up"* (Luke 18:1).

Once again, we must learn from the examples in the Bible. Dr. Wesley L. Duewel sheds some much needed insight on this subject:

"How long were the disciples to tarry in Jerusalem? *"Until you have been clothed with power from on high"* (Luke 24:49). How long did Moses keep his hands raised to God in prayer? Until Amalek was totally defeated (Exod. 17:13). How long did Joshua hold out his javelin toward Ai while the army attacked? Until Jericho was destroyed (Josh. 8:26). How long did Elijah stay on his knees in prevailing prayer after the three years' drought? Until rain clouds formed in the sky (1 Kings 18:44). How long did Jesus pray in Gethsemane? Until satan was defeated. How long did the disciples continue in prayer in the Upper Room? Until the Holy Spirit came upon them. No matter what our prayer request, if God has led us to pray for a need that we believe is the will of God, how long should we pray? Until the answer comes!"[51]

I have some great news. We have a beautiful promise directly from God that He will answer our prayers (1 John 5;14-15)

"Now this is the confidence that we have in Him, that if we ask anything according to His will, He hears us. 15 And if we know that He hears us, whatever we ask, we know that we have the petitions that we have asked of Him."

The above scripture is what drives the intercessor to petition God again and again. They knock and keep on knocking (Matthew 7:7). There is no timidity; there is justifiable assurance that God has heard and will grant their heart's desire. They know that He will answer!

E.M. Bounds said, "He prays not at all, who does not press his plea. Cold prayers have no claim on heaven, and no hearing in the courts above. Fire is the life of prayer, and heaven is reached by flaming importunity rising in an ascending scale."[52]

---

[51] Duewel, Wesley L.. Mighty Prevailing Prayer: Experiencing the Power of Answered Prayer (pp. 157-158). HarperCollins Christian Publishing. Kindle Edition.

[52] E.M. Bounds, *Necessity of Prayer*, 68.

Actually, I believe God looks at someone who refuses to accept *no* for an answer as someone who demonstrates great faith. The Lord loves it when we come again and again with our requests.

ADDED FUEL

When you want to faint, give up, and stop praying, meditate on these timeless promises from the Lord. He will answer you!

*"Call to Me, and I will answer you, and show you great and mighty things,
Which you do not know."*
Jeremiah 33:3

"Ask, and it shall be given...."
Matthew 7:7

"And all things, whatsoever you ask in prayer, believing you shall receive..."
Matthew 21:22

"But even now I know that whatever You ask of God, God will give You."
John 11:22

"And whatever you ask in My name, that I will do, that the Father may be glorified in the Son"
John 14:13

"Until now you have asked nothing in My name. Ask, and you will receive,   that your joy may be full."
John 16:24

21

LIQUID PRAYERS

*"When you know what time it is
you know what to do."*
Dutch Sheets

Robert Murray M'Cheyne, who lived only 29 years, was a Presbyterian minister who pastored a thriving church in Scotland and whose ministry greatly impacted the world. We find the secret to his success in one of his journal entries, "Sabbath. Rose early to seek God, and found Him whom my soul loveth. Who would not rise early to meet such company?"[53]

Once while addressing a young person who was studying for the ministry, M'Cheyne said, "Do everything in earnest. Above all, keep much in the presence of God. Never see the face of man

---

[53] Ibid.

till you have seen His face who is our life, our all."[54] What an amazing quest - see the face of God before you look into the face of man. No wonder this young man quickly advanced in favor with the Lord.

The story has often been told about a visitor who came to see Robert Murray M'Cheyne's church and pulpit after his death. The sexton took him to the pastor's office and, pointed to M'Cheyne's chair and said, "Sit there. Now put your elbows on the table." The visitor obeyed. "Now put your face in your hands." Again, the visitor complied. "Now let the tears flow. That was the way Mr. M'Cheyne used to do."

He then led the visitor to M'Cheyne's pulpit, where he had blessed the people by his ministry. "Put your elbows on the pulpit," said the old sexton. The visitor complied. "Put your face in your hands." Again, the visitor obeyed. "Now let the tears flow. That was the way Mr. M'Cheyne used to do." Ah, that was the secret of his ministry. He carried the burden of his people and of his nation and of God's cause upon his heart. Let the Holy Spirit burden you.[55]

---

[54] https://www.mcheyne.info/life.php

[55] Duewel, Wesley L. Mighty Prevailing Prayer: Experiencing the Power of Answered Prayer (p. 120). HarperCollins Christian Publishing. Kindle Edition.

ARE TEARS NECESSARY?

We have all heard the cliche statements "real men don't cry" or "big girls don't cry" or even "stop crying." These statements have caused many of us to look at crying as a character flaw that somehow reflects an inner weakness. Sadly, some are told that showing emotion and especially crying should be avoided at all times. Not only is this unbiblical, but it is unhealthy as well.

Let me say, not only has research proven that crying has multiple health benefits for us physically, but crying is also strongly encouraged in the Bible.

I believe a greater revelation is coming to the body of Christ regarding the power of tears in intercession. Yes, tears while we pray! When we weep before the Lord, we have affirmation from scripture that our tears have a voice. That is right, a voice…your tears speak!

"The Lord has heard the voice of my weeping."
Psalm 6:8

Think about the magnitude of the above verse. It should change how we view tears in prayer. Charles Spurgeon grasped the significance of his tears while in prayer, "My God, I will "weep" when I cannot plead, for You hear the *voice* of my weeping!"[56]

NEWS FLASH: Our tears are a special and precious type of intercession to God. I need you to see this - each tear that comes from your eyes, runs down your cheek and falls onto the floor - God not only sees them, but hears their voice, for they intercede for someone or something. The reason you are crying is important to God. Each tear is unique and renders a distinct prayer request before God. For example, you may be weeping over the spiritual condition of your children. Those tears have a voice and that voice is reaching the ears of God. Perhaps, the tears fall because of a situation that seems to be overwhelming, a problem, a burden, or maybe a lost soul trying to find God.

The tears that wet the altar, the table, or even the floor speak when we are at a loss for words, yes, but something else is also true. These tears can and often flow when we are fully engaged in vocalizing our prayers to the Lord. Therefore, God hears the prayers we are speaking, and at the same time, He hears the prayers that are falling from our eyes. This is miraculous and so powerful!

---

[56] https://www.gracegems.org/2013/08/liquid.html

HE SAID IT IS A CRIME

Wesley Duewel made one of the boldest statements ever on the importance of praying with compassion and passion,

> *"It is a **spiritual crime** to be calloused while the world goes to hell. It is spiritually criminal to pray casually, dry-eyed and burdenless, while a world is in sin and pain. It is Christ-like for your heart to weep with those who weep (Rom. 12:15). It is Christ-like for you to be so filled with loving compassion that you pray with tears for those broken, fettered, and destroyed by sin."*[57]

When we enter this realm of prayer, be encouraged. Why? This is a sign of greater spiritual sensitivity because you have tapped into the heart of the Father. You are being moved by what moves Him. It is an indication that you feel what He feels. It is also a sign of spiritual maturity, and you are actually entering into a new dimension of spiritual depth and power.

I wholeheartedly believe our liquid prayers flow directly into the deepest part of the heart of our Father. Now, let it be understood in this context I

---

[57] https://www.heraldofhiscoming.org/index.php/126-past-issues/2012/mar12/1610-lord-give-us-tears-as-we-pray-3-12

am not talking about "self-serving" tears where you are sad because your day didn't go as planned. No, I am talking about tears that flow due to the burden you feel and carry regarding the cause of Christ.

THERE IS A SHIFT COMING TO YOU

When you begin to capture the true essence of the Father's heart, you will begin to feel and think differently. You will become emotionally engaged. You will find yourself drawn into times and perhaps seasons of emotionally agonizing prayer. Currently, this type of prayer may be foreign to you, but when you align yourself with what the Father loves and desires to see happen, agonizing, groaning, and heartfelt intercession will knock on the door of your heart. Let me encourage you to embrace it and willingly move toward it. When you do, you will find yourself becoming burdened to the point of intercession over people who are far from God. Why? Because they matter deeply to Him. In addition, you will find yourself weeping over the carnality and coldness of the church. Why? On many occasions she has dismissed His ministry among them. Only then will nations, cultures, and the woes of the world will capture your heart as you see the brutality and horror of an eternity that awaits people who don't know Him. Prepare yourself for this prayer burden! It is coming to you, but you have to cooperate with it. Go ahead and give God your "yes."

YOU HAVE A HELPER

Remember, you are not alone in this time of intercession...Jesus will help you. Jesus said He would send us a "Helper." Remember, the Holy Spirit lives inside you and HE IS YOUR HELPER...this includes prayer! He will help you pray effectively. Again, Romans 8:26 reminds us that *"We don't know how to pray as we ought, **but the Holy Spirit makes** intercession...."* This is where true prayer comes alive - when the Holy Spirit helps us.

*"Likewise the Spirit also helps in our weaknesses. For we do not know what we should pray for as we ought, but the Spirit Himself makes intercession for us with **groaning** which cannot be utter."*
Romans 8:26

The word for "groan" in this verse is *stenagmos*. It is an inward groaning, a deep sigh, a heartfelt cry, a longing for divine deliverance. It can also express an inner languishing. When you are serious about initiating the cause of Christ there are moments you may be so troubled, vexed, or touched in your soul regarding a situation(s) that you can't accurately articulate or find the right words to say or pray. You are feeling the full weight of the issue and what comes out of your being is unintelligible utterances. When this happens rejoice. Why? God is highlighting a significant need, and He needs you to battle it out in prayer. He has chosen you to lead the way on this issue.

This is another level of intercession. I find it amazing that God understands every sound coming from our spirit, even when we don't. He precisely interprets our groans and unintelligible whispers. He even listens to the tears we shed.

> *"Those who sow in tears shall reap with shouts of joy!"*
> Psalm 126:5

Wesley L. Duewel listed 5 reasons we should weep before the Lord.[58]

* **We should weep because humanity has forsaken God!**

* **We should weep because sin is multiplying!**

---

[58] https://www.heraldofhiscoming.org/index.php/126-past-issues/2012/mar12/1610-lord-give-us-tears-as-we-pray-3-12

* **We should weep because as a church we are too lifeless and powerless!**

* **We should weep because we as God's people are spiritually asleep."**

* **We should weep because Christ's coming is so near and our task so incomplete!**

Let me encourage you to begin interceding on a regular basis for the items listed above. It is a beautiful place to start. By faith, boldly ask the Lord to give you His heart and concern for the above list. He will do it! Next, yield yourself to Him, and let the Holy Spirit pray through you over these issues.

22

THE UNSAVED IN YOUR LIFE

"I question if any believer can have the burden of souls upon him—a passion for souls—and not agonize in prayer."
Martin Luther

George Mueller began praying for five unsaved friends. After five years, one came to Christ. After ten more years of prayer, two more were converted. Three of the five were saved, two more were still on the list. Once Mueller said in Chicago, "I have prayed for two men by name every day for thirty-five years; on land or sea, sick or well, I have remembered them before God by name…. I shall continue to pray for them daily, by name, until they are saved, or die." After thirty-five years of prayer, the fourth was saved.

Mueller prayed almost fifty-two years, and the fifth was saved just after Mueller's death.[59]

What a shining example for us to follow. Mueller knew these men would spend an eternity apart from Christ unless they were born again. This motivated him to remain faithful in prayer. I am sure that he became discouraged at times, but he never stopped praying his friends.

HIS FINGERS ARE AROUND THEM

Praying for the unsaved is arduous work. It is a spiritual battle. Look at it this way - when you are interceding for an unsaved person, you are literally prying the fingers of satan off of them. Satan doesn't want to let them go, so he squeezes harder; he tightens his grip. He knows your prayers are a threat to him, so he tries to bring the person you are praying for into deeper deception and darkness. Be aware of these tactics, and whatever you do, don't stop praying!

Prepare yourself mentally, emotionally, and spiritually because there will be disappointments and setbacks. Again, it often seems that the more we pray for someone to be saved, the more they drift from God. And it appears they are become more engaged in sin and have no desire

---

[59] Charles A. Blanchard, *Getting Things From God* (Chicago: Moody, 1915), 128–29.

to make things right with God. If you see this happening, "double-down" on your prayer efforts. It is an indication God is at work.

When you pray in faith, God moves. Let me assure you no matter what you see and hear, rest assured God is working on your lost friends and loved ones. The Holy Spirit is convicting them of their sin and encouraging them to repent in order to have peace with God. On the other hand, be aware that satan is also working. This is why we must remain steadfast in praying for the unsaved. Eventually, if you do not give up, your prayers will remove the resisting spirits so that the heart can be receptive to the gospel (2 Corinthians 4:4).

BE ENCOURAGED!

It is quite possible the greatest contribution you can make toward someone salvation is to pray for them. I love what Sidlow Baxter said about praying for the lost. He said, "Men may spurn our appeals, reject our message, oppose our arguments, despise our persons, but they are helpless against our prayers."

Pay attention to the following examples of persistence in prayer. May we have the same determination to not give up. May we demonstrate a tenacious spirit in prayer that will not relent until the answer comes.

- William Carey, the great missionary to India, worked among and prayed for the Indian people for seven years before he baptized his first convert.

- Adoniram Judson poured his life out for the cause of Christ in Burma. He suffered greatly. He diligently prayed and worked among the Burmese people for seven years before he led his first person to Christ

- Robert Morrison, shortly after his arrival in China, was asked if he expected to have any spiritual impact on the Chinese. He answered, "No sir, but I expect God will!"[60] Morrison prayed and labored for seven years before he brought his first Chinese person to Christ.

- Robert Moffatt, who went to spread the gospel to the Bechunanas of South Africa, prayed and gave himself to the cause of Christ. He labored seven years before the Holy Spirit moved upon the people.

- Henry Richards also denied himself for the work of the cross. It took him seven years before he saw his first convert in the Congo.

---

[60] R.Li-Hua (2014. *Competivenes of Chinese Firms: West Meets East.* (Springer) p. 40

He never stopped praying. He knew his work was difficult but not in vain.[61]

These great men of God prayed diligently for a long time. They kept at it until God answered! May we learn from their example to never stop praying.

DELAY IS NOT A NO

I have to stress this point. Many of the requests made to God often don't get realized in our lives because of our lack of persistence in prayer. We give up too soon. We stop praying due to many factors. The main reason we stop is because we don't see immediate results. Proper understanding is essential moving forward. Delay in answered prayer is not necessarily resistance from heaven or a "NO" from God. It may be resistance from the devil. The devil wants to drag your loved one to hell and will use all capable means to resist the impact that your prayers are having.

These two scriptures should encourage you.

> "*Let us not become weary in doing good, for at the proper time, we will reap a harvest **if we do not give up**.*"
> Galatians 6:9,

[61] McIntyre, *Hidden Life of Prayer,* 87.

*"Men ought always to pray and **not give up**."*
Jesus (Luke 18:1)

I know you have been praying a long time for people that you love. Let me encourage you to take a deep breath and pray some more. Again, Jesus said in Luke 18:1, *"Men ought always to pray and **not give up**."* Each day that you pray it weakens the enemy. You are making a huge difference. Don't forget people have had years to develop their world view, sin habits, and beliefs. Satan is often deeply entrenched, and it will take time to dig him out of the holes he has a legal right to. Remember, you are at war!

Right now, place the book down and ask the Holy Spirit to lead you as you pray for the unsaved people in your life. Call each person by name and pray as the Spirit of God leads you. Remember, with every whisper to God on their behalf, you are prying satan's devious fingers off of their life.

23

WHY I DON'T WANT TO PRAY

"All vital praying makes a drain on a man's vitality. True intercession is a sacrifice, a bleeding sacrifice."
J.H. Jewett

I don't think I am the only one who feels the need to improve their prayer life. Even to this day I don't think I am where I need to be. Each day, the voice in my spirit echoes, "When will we pray?" My flesh wants to make excuses, but my spirit knows that my effectiveness is connected to my moments with God.

THE STRUGGLE IS REAL

Over the years I have learned the simple truth about prayer: the struggle to pray is real; it never gets easy. There are so many distractions, demands, and obstacles to overcome. It takes discipline and an uncompromising resolve to "give yourself to prayer."

Below are some embedded themes that keep many from fully embracing prayer.

However, before I list them, let the wise words of A.A. Bonar encourage you to reject the resistance to pray. He said, "O brother, pray; in spite of Satan, pray; spend hours in prayer; rather neglect friends than not pray; rather fast, and lose breakfast, dinner, tea, and supper—and sleep —than not pray. And we must not talk about prayer, we must pray with purpose and sincerity. The Lord is near. He comes quietly while the bridesmaids sleep."[62]

I don't know about you, but what Bonar said inspires me to want to pray. However, each day is a new battle.

Here it is: are you ready? Over the next couple of chapters, I will share three reasons why Christians don't seriously pray.

In my experience, the following is the main reason Christians don't pray fervently. **"GOD IS**

---

[62] David McIntyre The Hidden Life of Prayer (GodliPress Classics on How to Pray) (p. 66). GodliPress. Kindle Edition.

GOING TO DO WHATEVER HE WANTS TO DO ANYWAY." Many believe their prayers really don't matter because they have relentlessly been told that God controls and predetermines all the activities and outcomes surrounding our lives. The net result is that we simply disengage from the discipline of prayer. In all honestly, it is difficult to be committed to prayer when you believe that everything is already predetermined. Why waste the energy and time if God has already made up His mind?

Let me help you navigate through the above mindset.

Look at prayer this way - Biblical praying is partnering OR co-laboring with God to get His will done on the earth. Take a look at the first part of 2 Corinthians 6:1 *"We then, as workers together **with Him**..."* The Greek word for *"workers together"* is *synergeō*. It means to help, to labor, to work together, to assist, to put forth power together. We get our word "synergy" from this word. Don't forget it was the infamous John Wesley that said, "God does nothing except in response to believing prayer." So, God *does* need us to pray, and in fact, He *allows* our prayers to determine much of His activity on the earth.

Elisabeth Elliot, who was the wife of missionary Jim Elliott, was killed in 1956 while attempting to minister to the Auca people of eastern Ecuador.

She said, "Prayer lays hold of God's plan and becomes the link between His will and accomplishments on earth. Amazing things happen, and we are given the privilege of being the channels of the Holy Spirit's prayer."

People of prayer know and fully understand that prayer influences God and His movements. Being a believer is more than being a silent partner where we observe from the sidelines while God does all the heavy lifting. The scriptures are pretty clear and reveal that we actually get to partner with Him and be a significant contributor to the workings of God. This placement is not just for the spiritual elite. No, it is for us all. God invites us into this strategic alignment.

SECOND REASON WE DON'T PRAY

Prayer, for many seems like a hopeless exercise. If we are honest, there is a level of frustration that can accompany anyone who attempts to be consistent in prayer. This leads me to the second reason believers struggle in the area of prayer: **they have sincerely asked God for specific request and are disappointed by the lack of response from the Lord.**

I am sure all of us have been affected by God's denial or delay. This can affect your drive to pray.

Oftentimes, people simply give up. They feel rejected, unheard, and even neglected.

Many can identify with Job and what he said while he was walking through the catastrophic events that took place in his life. He said,

"What would we gain by praying to Him?"
Job 21:15

This begs the question, "What do we do when God hasn't answered our prayers?"

Often, when the answer doesn't come on our time-table, we pull back and stop praying for that issue. This is a big mistake, and it plays right into the enemy's hands. The devil's goal is for you to become discouraged and exasperated to the point that you don't even contend any more. Remember, there is a resistance to every Kingdom request you make of the Father. Our responsibility is to not give up! Our responsibility in prayer is to keep believing, to stand firm, and to pray until your requests manifest.

THE LIGHT BULB COMES ON

The rest of this chapter is going to change your prayer life. Let's start with what John Calvin wrote regarding what to do when you don't receive an immediate answer to your prayer(s). He said, "We must repeat the same supplication not twice or three times only but as often as we have need, a hundred and a thousand times.... We must never be weary in waiting for God's help."[63]

To help you understand this concept further, E.M. Bounds said, "We must not only pray, but we must pray with great urgency, with intentness and with repetition. We must not only pray, but we must pray again and again.... Jesus made it very plain that the secret of prayer and its success lie in its urgency."[64]

JUDGE AND NEIGHBOR

On more than one occasion, Jesus spoke straightforwardly about prevailing persistent prayer. One such place is Luke 18.

This parable isn't comparing God to the unjust judge, for God is not unjust in any way; the central theme of Luke 18 is that one should NOT LOSE HEART while praying. Luke stresses this point in verse one.

---

[63] Donald G. Bloesch, *Struggle of Prayer*, (Colorado Springs: Helmers and Howard, 1988), 80

[64] E.M Bounds, *Purpose in Prayer*, 55.

---

*"Then He spoke a parable to them, that men always ought to pray and not lose heart, **2** saying: "There was in a certain city a judge who did not fear God nor regard man. **3** Now there was a widow in that city; and she came to him, saying, 'Get justice for me from my adversary.' 4 And he would not for a while; but afterward he said within himself, 'Though I do not fear God nor regard man, **5** yet because this widow troubles me I will avenge her, lest by her continual coming she weary me.'**6** " Then the Lord said, "Hear what the unjust judge said. **7** And shall God not avenge His own elect who cry out day and night to Him, though He bears long with them?"*

In verse 5, in the middle of the parable, Jesus makes a striking comment about the tenacity of this lady… *"Yet because this widow troubles me I will avenge her, lest by her continual coming she weary me.'"*

This lady had obviously been taken advantage of by her adversary. All she wanted was for justice to be done, and the judge was the only one with the power to do so. When the judge didn't respond to her requests, she didn't quit trying to receive justice for her cause. She earnestly kept asking.

Jesus used two key phrases, to discuss what persistent praying is about: *"Troubles me"* and *"continually coming she weary me."* These phrases are in the context of effective praying.

Why did Jesus choose these specific words in this parable? I believe Jesus wanted us to understand that prayer is more than casually asking one time. Prayer is about believing and having a resolve to not give up. This lady remained steadfast in her pursuit of justice until the answer arrived. She was persistent, tenacious, and annoying all at the same time. This is a key kingdom principle.

I believe we can safely assume that some answers to prayer do not manifest because we give up praying too soon.

24

MY FLESH SAYS "NO!"

"Some people think God does not like to be troubled with our constant coming and asking. The way to trouble God is not to come at all."
Dwight L. Moody

Charles Spurgeon challenges us to remember where we are when we pray. He said, "When we pray, we are standing in the palace, on the glittering floor of the great King's own reception room, and thus we are placed upon a vantage ground. In prayer we stand where angels bow with veiled faces; there, even there, the cherubim and seraphim adore, before that selfsame throne to which our prayers ascend."[65]

---

[65] Charles Haddon Spurgeon, *Twelve Sermons on Prayer* (London: Marshall, Morgan & Scott, n.d.), 60.

Oh my! Think about the privilege we have to draw near and share our heart to the One who measures the universe between His pinky finger and His thumb (Isaiah 40:12). This One, who uses the earth as a footstool, invites us to come boldly before His throne of grace and to ask for help (Isaiah 66:1; Hebrews 4:16).

CONFESSION TIME

If we are honest, our flesh isn't attracted to prayer. This the third reason we don't want to pray. Our flesh fights it; I know mine does.

ALSO, many come to me and say, "I want to pray, but I DON'T KNOW HOW TO PRAY!" Is this you?

Well, welcome to the number of people who don't know how to pray. Here is a valuable truth…You learn to fight by fighting! You learn to swim by swimming. And, you learn to pray by praying. You don't wake up one day as a senior commander in the prayer army of God. Your effectiveness in prayer increases the more you pray. There is no short cut, nor is there a quick seminar that thoroughly equips you to be a giant on your knees. It only comes through "doing" prayer.

John Laidlaw gave some great advice when he said, "The main lesson about prayer is just this:

Do it! Do it! Do it! You want to be taught to pray. My answer is: Pray and never faint, and then you shall never fail."[66] This is fabulous advice! *Do it! Do it! Do it!*

Physically you don't get "into shape" by going to the gym occasionally, you get into shape by being consistent and disciplined. It is the same with your prayer muscles - use them and use them often.

Duewel Wesley wrote, "Prevailing prayer was His lifelong vocation. All that Christ accomplished during His earthly ministry was born in intercession, covered and saturated with intercession, and empowered and anointed as a result of intercession."[67] Jesus is our example for prevailing prayer.

READ THE SMALL PRINT

I know you are getting inspired to pray, but be warned the flesh will almost always resist and look for other things to do. By much experience, you know that the flesh dislikes discipline. It

---

[66] David McIntyre The Hidden Life of Prayer (GodliPress Classics on How to Pray) (p. 66). GodliPress. Kindle Edition.

[67] Duewel, Wesley L. Mighty Prevailing Prayer: Experiencing the Power of Answered Prayer (p. 39). HarperCollins Christian Publishing. Kindle Edition.

---

seeks comfort and pleasure, and prayer is anything but comfortable. It is a sacrifice and at times painful.

David McIntyre nailed it when he described a believer's struggle to pray consistently. Be forewarned, you are about to get a dose of true genuine uncomfortable transparency.

> "Somebody who prayed often said, 'As for my heart, when I go to pray, I find it hates to go to God, and when it is with Him, hates to stay with Him, that many times I am forced in my prayers, first to beg of God that He would take my heart, and set it on Himself in Christ, and when it is there, that He would keep it there. Many times I don't know what to pray for, I am so blind, nor how to pray, I am so ignorant; only the Spirit helps our infirmities."[68]

And John Bunyan said regarding his own deep experiences with prayer, "Oh! the loopholes that the heart has in the time of prayer; none knows how many detours the heart has and back-lanes to slip away from the presence of God."[69]

---

[68] David McIntyre, *The Hidden Life of Prayer* (GodliPress Classics on How to Pray) (p. 26). GodliPress. Kindle Edition.

[69] David McIntyre, *The Hidden Life of Prayer* (GodliPress Classics on How to Pray) (p. 26). GodliPress. Kindle Edition.

I don't know about you, but I identify with every word these two men shared. I have discovered that to be faithful in prayer is the most difficult discipline of my life. My flesh makes every attempt possible to avoid the isolation, and once there, a myriad of reasons surf through my mind in attempt to pull me away from His presence. In all honesty, there are times I literally have to force myself to meet with God. Why? I would rather do anything but be still and wait on a God; at times, I do not see, nor feel, or hear Him speak.

Corey Russell, who in my opinion is one of the contemporary leading authorities on prayer, said, "The only way to persevere in prayer is to burn every other bridge."

Are you willing to burn the bridges?

HERE IS THE KEY!

Pay close attention to what Wesley Duewel states as he articulates what it will take to become disciplined for prayer. "The Holy Spirit does not tap you on the shoulder each morning, lift you out of bed, and place you on your knees. He does not rearrange your schedule so you have time for adequate prayer. You will have to discipline yourself. You will have to choose to have a life of prayer, a disciplined habit of prayer. If you cannot even do that much, don't talk about taking up your cross and following Jesus. Perhaps you are following Him at a distance, like Peter before he denied his Lord" (Matthew. 26:58).[70]

---

[70] Duewel, Wesley L.. *Mighty Prevailing Prayer: Experiencing the Power of Answered Prayer* (p. 227). HarperCollins Christian Publishing. Kindle Edition.

25

WHAT HAPPENS IN THE DARK DOESN'T STAY IN THE DARK

"The greatest enemy to the work of God is not Jezebal, a demon or the devil himself. It is the neglect of prayer. Nothing can stop a prayer empowered church!"
Todd Smith

There are multiple scenes in the Old Testament where Moses would enter the tabernacle, or tent of meeting to meet with God face-to-face (Exodus 33:8f). The Bible says that God talked to Moses like a friend. When Moses walked toward the tent, the people of Israel paid close attention, for they knew something consequential was about to take place. Moses would lower himself into the tent and sit before the Lord, and they would talk. Sometimes they would talk for hours and, on some occasions, even days.

Can you imagine listening to God speak to you face to face? Can you imagine hearing words from God's very own mouth? I don't know how Moses survived the meetings. Moses and God dialogued together. I am sure there were times Moses wept uncontrollably. I am sure there were times when he felt like he was going to die due to his proximity to perfect holiness and unfiltered glory. I am sure there were times when Moses worshipped extravagantly, and, oh yes, cried out for more of God's weighty glory. And then there were moments when Moses raised his doubts, questioning God's timing and intentions.

Moses also would bring up his concerns about the people God asked him to lead. Make no mistake about it, there was something special happening in the enclosure, beyond the eyes of Joshua and the inquiring people. Business was being done, but not just ordinary business. Business that involved a nation, history, and future generations. In fact, all of the world is still feeling the impact of what happened underneath that tent.

DO YOU HAVE A TENT?

In his book, *Practicing the Presence of God* Brother Lawrence states, "…You have to make a clear decision to stay consciously in God's presence. You must 'from this very moment, make a holy and firm resolution never to be willfully separated from Him, and to live the rest of your days in His sacred presence."[71]

Again, I ask do you have a "tent" where you meet with God? Since the vision of fire on the water and the glory resting at Christ Fellowship, I have traveled a great deal telling the story of the North Georgia Revival. My busy schedule attempts to rob me of my time with the Lord. However, to combat this, I have made the commitment that when I am in a hotel room the first thing that I do in the morning is place a towel on the bathroom floor and spend an hour with the Lord praying in tongues. The bathroom is my "tent of meeting." It becomes my "closet" as Jesus described in Matthew 6. While in the secret place, I purposely place my nose on the towel and speak to Him. I choose the bathroom because I can place my face next to the toilet - this is a stark reminder that I am nothing, and He is everything. I have to stay low. It is here that God hears my heart, and I attempt to capture His.

---

[71] Hansen, Gary Neal. Kneeling with Giants (p. 129). InterVarsity Press. Kindle Edition.

It is noteworthy to read what Lawrence says about his personal prayer time with the Father. He writes, "Sometimes I think of myself as a block of stone before a sculptor, ready to be sculpted into a statue, presenting myself thus to God and I beg Him to form His perfect image in my soul and make me entirely like himself."[72]

During your life, you will walk through many doors, but none is more sacred than this one - the door to your prayer closet. It's not a fancy door, nor should it be. In fact, it is quite ordinary and borderline unbecoming, basic, and bland. There are no flashing lights over the door, but the door does have a voice. It calls and begs you to step inside, for it knows the value of what takes place when you cross the threshold and close the door behind you.

Provision and power are found behind the door. Strength and strategy are there. Untold riches are there. Wisdom and weight (God's Glory) are there. Understanding and clarification are dispersed inside the closet. Sounds great, doesn't it? Well, there is more to reveal about what is on the other side of the door to the prayer closet.

THE OTHER SIDE OF THE COIN

---

[72] Ibid. p. 130

All the above is factual and experiential, but I must give you the full truth. The other side of the door is also a dreadful place. Why? Death happens behind the door. Doubt manifests there. Fears manifest there. Test results are revealed there. Pain happens there. Hips get dislocated, shoes come off, hair turns grey, voices get altered, and names get changed there. It's not an ivory cathedral, padded and pleasant; no, it's an old tent, a barn, a closet, a bathroom floor, and sometimes a garage. When you go inside, you notice there is a stench about the room because there is an invisible altar of fire. The smell of burnt flesh is never pleasant. It is here, in this place of meeting, that our bodies, our will, and our dreams are laid upon the altar. And it is here that they all die.

It is here that God does His greatest and most necessary work on us. His finger touches us. His scapula cuts us. His hand heals us. His voice guides us. His Spirit comforts us. His fire burns us.

If I am completely honest, and you know this already, the closet is a place of deep struggle. For instance, the dark room has a sound like no other – a deafening silence. A war rages on the inside; not a small skirmish, but an actual war. There are moments when we are in a wrestling match with principalities over our families, churches, and communities. In the closet, demonic spirits from various ranks are addressed and commanded to leave. While the battle can be contentious, a great deal of the time the war is internal. The battle in your mind and soul can be dreadful and even exhausting. I have struggled to conquer myself while in the darkness. I have struggled with my own fears, doubts, and worries. The agony and inner strife incessantly pull on me to leave the closet prematurely.

BUT! BUT! BUT! Here is the good news. What happens there in the closet is also otherworldly. When I persevere and meet with God, externally, impossible mountains begin to move. Strongholds become weaker; the devil loosens his grip, and I am more empowered to accomplish His wishes. Internally, a glorious transformation takes place in my heart and mind. It is in the quiet place that you will hear his whisper - that still small voice. You will receive the courage to conquer. You will come forth empowered and poised for the work of God at hand. You will enlarge your capacity and qualify yourself for greater work. It is here you will develop a personal history with God.

BEFORE THE EARTHQUAKE HITS

Here is why we must meet with God. Behind the closet door is the **HYPOCENTER** of all things. Become familiar with this word. It matters. Before an earthquake manifests on the earth, known as the epicenter, it first starts beneath the surface called the hypocenter. DON'T MISS THIS: An earthquake starts in the dark and then it breaks forth with unmatched and uncontainable force on the surface. An earthquake shakes, breaks, and repositions things. It can have a devastating effect on all who are impacted by it.

Again, just on the other side of two and half inches, the thickness of the door is HYPOCENTER!!! It is what separates you from His glory, His revival, and His power. The distance is small, but the step through it is massive. What happens behind the door will shake, break, and reposition things in the spirit as well as in the natural. Your obedience to get there and to pray will have devastating effect on the kingdom of darkness and at the same time release the purposes of God around you.

We have to master this door. Don't fear it, dread it, avoid it, live without it, excuse yourself from it, or assign others to it. To avoid it or neglect it serves our own defeat. Be faithful opening the door into the dark because nothing of eternal significance happens until it first happens in there.

26

LET IT RAIN!

*"When I pray, I assist the Lord in His endeavors.
I partner with the Him by joining myself
to His causes by operating in the greatest
ministry given to man, prayer."*
Todd Smith

The driest place on earth might surprise you - Atacama Desert, Chile. It is the most rainless place on the planet with average yearly precipitation of 0.03" (0.08 cm). In fact, there is a section of the Atacama Desert where no rainfall has ever been recorded.[73] I had no idea! The land is barren and dry with very little to no life. It would have to be a miserable existence to live in such dry and waterless conditions.

As I travel abroad and minister in various churches and denominations, I get a close look

---

[73] https://wmo.asu.edu/content/world-longest-recorded-dry-period#:~:text=Discussion,in%20the%20Atacama%20Desert%2C%20Chile.

at the overall health of the body of Christ. At times, I am encouraged, and at other moments, I am concerned. Regardless, I believe all of us would agree that we need a down pour of the Holy Spirit in our lives, our nation and our churches. However, just *wanting* it isn't enough. *More* is needed to open up the heavens.

HERE IS WHAT I KNOW

Without consistent fervent prevailing prayer, we are bankrupt of power. Our ministries, outreaches, and church services are utterly worthless without prayer. They simply have no kingdom weight, nor are they of any eternal value. I don't want to seem harsh or come across as critical, but without prayer we are clanging symbols that reach the ears only. Jude 12 says such empty teaching and ministry without Kingdom expression are literally "*clouds without rain.*"

If we take an honest evaluation and are completely truthful, the failures of the modern church can be traced back to our failure to pray fervently. I know we are quick to blame the culture, the devil, Jezebel, religious spirits, circumstances, and even others for lack of power. However, our failure boils down to this fact. Are we praying, and are we praying effectively?

What does fervent prevailing prayer look like? We get a glimpse of it in the following examples.

BLIND MAN HEALED

Blind Bartimaeus is a prime example of fervent prevailing prayer. He received word that a man, Jesus, had performed mighty miracles, including opening the eyes of the blind, was coming his way. Therefore, Blind Bartimaeus concluded that if Jesus gave one man his sight, then he was a candidate for Jesus to do it again. This was Bartimaeus' posture of faith! He incessantly cried out for Jesus' intervention (Mark 10:46–52). In fact, the text says, "He [Bartimaeus] began to shout, 'Jesus, Son of David, have mercy on me!'" The text implies that Bartimaeus called out until the Master responded. The end result was that Jesus came, touched His eyes, and Bartimaeus received his sight.

BLEEDING STOPPED

Do you recall the women with the issue of blood? Here is a beautiful example of the mentality necessary for fervent prevailing prayer. She heard of the miracles that Jesus had done for others, and rightly assumed that if He healed others, then He could also heal her. She didn't wait patiently for things to simply "work out." No, she had a fierceness about her - an adamant uncompromising mindset that prompted her to take action. She knew the crowds would be daunting and there would be great risks involved, but none of the negative details deterred her. She knew that if she touched Him, all would change for her.

There is an inward tenacity that you must possess if you are going to commit to pray this way. It takes an uncommon resolve to keep praying when everything around you screams, "You can't do this!" " Stop, you are wasting your time," or, "He will never answer you."

IT STARTED TO RAIN

The epic story of Elijah praying until it started to rain is another vivid example of fervent prevailing prayer. Elijah positioned himself at the top of Mount Carmel where he cried out for God to send rain. However, the rain didn't begin to fall the moment that Elijah asked God for rain. It took time, effort and much prayer before the first drops leaked from the clouds. The Biblical text actually reveals that Elijah prayed multiple times, and after each segment of prayer, he sent a servant to go outside to see if it was indeed raining. Each time the servant returned with a negative report of no rain.

Without question, Elijah fully expected it to rain at any moment, but it didn't. Elijah kept praying. In fact, he placed his face between his knees and interceded with greater intensity. It is interesting to note that he was in a birthing position. He sent the servant out again to see if it was raining, and it wasn't; however, the report from the servant was different. He came back running and announced, "A cloud is forming." The cloud was "off in the distance" and "the size of a man's hand."

The cloud wasn't there previously and now it was! But it still wasn't raining. Shortly thereafter, the heavens released its liquid gold - a torrential downpour occurred that blessed the whole nation. Note that the rains didn't fall until Elijah prayed seven times. (1 Kings 18:41-19:8; James 5:13f)

What if Elijah would have stopped praying? What if he didn't persevere past the fatigue, unanswered prayer, and the disappointment of delay? He could have said that he tried. After praying two or three times, he could have concluded that it must not have been God's will to send rain. However, Elijah knew God's will in this situation, and it was his responsibility to clear the way for the rain to fall to the earth. Take note, for this is important! Elijah knew what God wanted to do, but knowing wasn't enough! He prayed rain into existence! He pulled the rain down through prayer. Elijah prevailed in prayer, and a mighty force was released that saved a nation.

What do we learn from Elijah? Keep praying until the heaven opens.

ONE OF TWO THINGS

The difference between normal praying and fervent prevailing prayer is this: prevailing praying stays with an issue, item, or concern until one of two things happen:

> 1) The answer manifests in the natural. You see the answer with your eyes. In other words, the answer to your prayers is visible.

> 2) There is a note of peace in your heart, with Holy Spirit assurance, that heaven has heard your petition, and the answer is on the way.

MILITANT CHURCH

Ole Hallesby, a Lutheran Theologian once said, "God has voluntarily made himself dependent also upon our prayer.... In prayer the church has received power to rule the world. Through our prayers God acts and speaks. While God is ever free and acts in sovereign freedom, yet He seems to have bound Himself, at least to a large degree, to our intercession."[74]

We can no longer afford to admire our position of blessing and prosperity alone. The times in which we live demand a more militant position. We are in an epic battle for the soul of the world. In reality, we are at war for God.

The church must see herself differently these days. God is leaning into us. He longs to hear our intercession. Fervent prevailing prayer has to be embraced by the body of Christ. The work of God depends upon it. If we fail here, a detrimental impact on the cause of Christ in our churches and around the world will take place.

However, if we commit ourselves to this most important work the world will experience an an awakening of which the world has never seen.

We are a part of the solution, we can make a difference. Embrace the challenge and give yourself to prayer.

Heaven awaits your response!

---

[74] O. Hallesby, Prayer (London: Hodder & Stoughton, 1936), 229, 231; see also Donald G. Bloesch, The Struggle of Prayer (San Francisco: Harper, 1980), 87–88.